T0329148

Cambridge Elements ≡

Elements in Public Policy
edited by
M. Ramesh
National University of Singapore
Michael Howlett
National University of Singapore
David L. Weimer
University of Wisconsin – Madison
Xun Wu
Hong Kong University of Science and Technology
Judith Clifton
University of Cantabria
Eduardo Araral
National University of Singapore

HOW IDEAS AND INSTITUTIONS SHAPE THE POLITICS OF PUBLIC POLICY

Daniel Béland
McGill University, Montreal

CAMBRIDGE
UNIVERSITY PRESS

CAMBRIDGE
UNIVERSITY PRESS

University Printing House, Cambridge CB2 8BS, United Kingdom

One Liberty Plaza, 20th Floor, New York, NY 10006, USA

477 Williamstown Road, Port Melbourne, VIC 3207, Australia

314–321, 3rd Floor, Plot 3, Splendor Forum, Jasola District Centre,
New Delhi – 110025, India

79 Anson Road, #06–04/06, Singapore 079906

Cambridge University Press is part of the University of Cambridge.

It furthers the University's mission by disseminating knowledge in the pursuit of
education, learning, and research at the highest international levels of excellence.

www.cambridge.org
Information on this title: www.cambridge.org/9781108721837
DOI: 10.1017/9781108634700

First published 2019

A catalogue record for this publication is available from the British Library.

ISBN 978-1-108-72183-7 Paperback
ISSN 2398-4058 (online)
ISSN 2514-3565 (print)

How Ideas and Institutions Shape the Politics of Public Policy

Elements in Public Policy

DOI: 10.1017/9781108634700
First published online: May 2019

Daniel Béland
Mcgill University, Montreal
Author for correspondence: Daniel Béland, daniel.beland@mcgill.ca

Abstract: This Element provides a critical review of existing literature on the role of ideas and institutions in public policy, with the aim of contributing to the study of the politics of public policy. Because most policy scholars deal with the role of ideas or institutions in their research, such a critical review should help them improve their knowledge of crucial analytical issues in policy and political analysis. The discussion brings together insights from both the policy studies literature and new institutionalism in sociology and political science, and stresses the explanatory role of ideas and institutions.

Keywords: public policy, ideas, institutions, institutionalism, politics

ISBNs: 9781108721837 (PB), 9781108634700 (OC)
ISSNs: 2398-4058 (online), 2514-3565 (print)

Contents

1 Introduction

Public policy is largely the product of political factors that require a systematic examination. Much has been written recently about how two of types of factors – ideas and institutions - can shape the politics of public policy (e.g., Béland 2009; Béland and Waddan 2012; Campbell 2004; Lieberman 2002; Orenstein 2008; Peters, Pierre, and King 2005; Schmidt 2011; Walsh 2000). This double emphasis on ideas and institutions is hardly surprising as it is present in the history of social science research going back to the work of Max Weber (1978), who is perceived as one of the key precursors of modern ideational and institutional analysis (Lepsius 2017). Revisiting this ideational and institutional tradition is helpful to grasp the politics of public policy, which is a key challenge for contemporary policy studies, including theories of the policy process (Weible and Sabatier 2018).

Beginning with historical institutionalism, a theoretical perspective centred on the historical analysis of institutions, this Element provides a critical review of some of the existing literature on the role of ideas and institutions in the politics of public policy. The aim is to contribute to comparative policy analysis and, more generally, the study of the politics of public policy, which is a crucial yet sometimes neglected issue in policy studies. Because most policy scholars interested in politics deal, in one way or another, with the role of ideas or institutions in their research, such a critical review should help them improve their knowledge of crucial analytical issues in policy and political analysis. The ensuing discussion brings together insights from both the policy studies literature and new institutionalism in sociology and political science, and stresses the explanatory role of ideas and institutions while directly engaging with existing approaches.

This Element addresses key issues for the study of policy stability and change: the relationship among different types of explanations in social science and public policy research, and the potential effects of their interaction and potential interdependence; the role of ideational and institutional processes in the construction of key policy actors' preferences and perceived interests; the role of ideas across the policy cycle and across territorial boundaries, and especially the role of transnational actors; and, finally, asymmetrical power relations among policy actors and how these relations affect the politics of ideas – in particular, institutional settings.

Now that we know what this contribution is about, it is helpful to explain what it is *not* about. First, this study focuses primarily on theoretical rather than methodological issues. Simultaneously, this Element recognizes that different methods, such as process tracing and quantitative analysis, can be used to explore the role of ideas and their interaction with institutions (Béland and Cox 2011b; Jacobs 2015). Second, because of the limited space available, this Element does not systematically review all the literatures relevant for the analysis of ideational and institutional processes in political and policy research. Instead, it discusses the selected approaches because they illustrate key theoretical issues for the study of ideas and institutions in public policy. More detailed literature reviews on specific topics are already available, and many are cited in this Element to allow the reader to learn more about particular topics as needed.

Although this Element is largely theoretical in nature, it features selected examples and is written in a way that should make it accessible to a broad array of scholars. Written primarily for students and researchers, it should also be accessible to practitioners and informed readers. This Element covers a lot of theoretical ground and its structure is as straightforward as it can be considering the sheer number of issues at hand. In total, sixteen short sections comprise this Element: the Introduction, fourteen substantive sections, and the Conclusion. What these substantive sections have in common is that they each help the reader attain a better grasp of the politics of public policy through the consideration of key theoretical issues.

After this Introduction, we outline what ideas and institutions mean (Section 2). Then, attention turns more systematically to the widely used yet ambiguous and contested concept of institutionalism (Section 3). This is followed by a discussion of political institutions (Section 4) and policy feedback (Section 5) as they are studied within historical institutionalism, the type of institutionalism that is most centred on politics, political institutions, and policy legacies. Attention then turns to the role of ideas within historical institutionalism (Section 6) and, more specifically, to the different types of ideas considered in the literature (Section 7). Then, we map the role of ideas and the actors carrying them across the policy cycle (Section 8). This mapping exercise leads to a critical look at existing theories of the policy process, with a focus on the advocacy coalition and the multiple-streams frameworks, both of which have a number of limitations as far as the combined and systematic study of ideas and institutions is concerned (Section 9). This is followed by a discussion of analytical issues particularly relevant for the combined examination of ideas and institutions: the role of transnational actors (Section 10), the construction of identities (Section 11), the politics of interests as it relates to inequalities and asymmetrical power relations (Section 12), the production of expertise (Section 13), the mechanisms of policy change (Section 14) and, finally, the potential impact of psychological and structural factors as they relate to ideational and institutional factors (Section 15). The Conclusion

(Section 16) sketches an agenda for future research about the relationship between ideas and institutions in the politics of public policy.

A key take-away message of this Element is that combining the study of ideas and institutions in the analysis of policy stability and change requires researchers to draw a clear analytical line between them before exploring how these two types of explanation may interact or even become interdependent. This task requires breaking down ideas and institutions while taking into account other potential explanations, namely structural and psychological ones.

2 Ideas and Institutions as Explanatory Factors

One of the most crucial tasks necessary for the development of both ideational and institutional analysis is to understand "ideas" and "institutions" as distinct explanatory factors in policy and political research. We can rely on the work of Craig Parsons (2007) to do this. Parsons convincingly maps explanatory arguments in the context of a simple yet compelling typology (for a critical discussion of his work, see Daigneault and Béland 2015).

Parsons (2007) identifies four main logics of explanation in political and policy research: structural, institutional, ideational, and psychological. First, structural and institutional explanations feature a logic-of-position that "explains by detailing the landscape around someone to show how an obstacle course of material or man-made constraints and incentives channels her to certain actions" (Parsons 2007, p. 13). Here, the term "structural" points to exogenous material explanations and "institutional" refers to historically constructed explanations. Second, ideational and psychological explanations feature a logic-of-interpretation that "explains by showing that someone arrives at an action only through one interpretation of what is possible and/or desirable" (Parsons 2007, p. 13). The main difference between ideational and psychological explanations is that the former are historically contingent while the later reflect hardwired cognitive processes.

This typology is useful for ideational and institutional analysis in part because it helps elucidate how scholars can combine the logic-of-position associated with institutions and the logic-of-interpretation associated with ideas. From this perspective, we should first draw a clear line between ideas and institutions before assessing how they might shape the behaviour and decisions of individual and collective actors, separately or in tandem, through interaction effects or even through what Tasleem Padamsee (2009, p. 427) calls the "interdependence" of explanatory factors. "Interdependence" occurs when such factors become so intertwined that their respective policy impact depends on their mutual imbrication. For instance, in the United States during the New Deal, the payroll tax as a policy instrument became inseparable from both the then limited institutional fiscal capacity of the federal government (Leff 1983) and the idea of social insurance that President Franklin Delano Roosevelt had long embraced (Richards 1994). Here, the push for payroll tax funding as part of the 1935 Social Security Act became the product of these two factors, as they proved closely intertwined and interdependent in their capacity to shape policy change (Béland 2007a).

As this discussion suggests, both ideas and institutions are likely to interact, or even become interdependent, to shape human behaviours and decisions, but the weight of each type of explanation and the ways in which ideas and institutions interact is contingent. This means that assessing their respective roles and potential relationships is an empirical question.

Simultaneously, although scholars might first look at ideas and institutions and the ways in which they might interact to shape how actors behave, they should also realize that turning to ideas and institutions and their interaction in their own right might not always be sufficient to explain particular human behaviours and institutions. This is why, when ideational and institutional factors fail to explain key outcomes, scholars should take a closer look at psychological and structural factors and assess whether they provide better explanations either on their own or combined with one another. This is consistent with Parsons' (2007) urging for scholars to start with their preferred types of explanation before turning to other causal factors, if necessary. This is why although the primary focus of this Element is on ideational and institutional processes, we take a more systematic look at psychological and structural factors as a way to remind the reader about the potential explanatory importance of these factors (Section 15).

Throughout this Element, the term "ideas" simply refers to the historically constructed beliefs and perceptions of both individual and collective actors. The emphasis on actors is crucial here because the best ideational analysis always begins and ends with the ways in which concrete actors think and talk about the world. This is true for two main reasons. First, ideational analysis recognizes the agency of social and political actors in shaping and reshaping policy ideas and discourse (Hay 2011; for a more general discussion on agency and public policy, see Capano and Galanti 2018). Second, detaching ideas from the discourse through which they are communicated makes ideas look overly abstract and detached from concrete political and policy interactions (Schmidt 2008). From this perspective, focusing on the actual actors who articulate key ideas over time is an appropriate way to avoid idealism in the pejorative sense of the term (Béland and Cox 2011b).

The close link between ideas and actors leads us to study institutions, which refers to embedded rules and norms that shape these actors' behaviours alongside, and in conjunction with, ideas. Institutions are social and political settlements and the products of power struggles (Campbell 2004, p. 1), which are themselves embedded in ideational and institutional processes (Béland 2010b; Carstensen and Schmidt 2016).

Ideas and institutions are closely related simply because actors' beliefs and perceptions can later become institutions, which are the rules of the game that both constrain and empower actors in various settings. Although they are associated with the logic-of-position (Parsons 2007), in the social and political world institutions are subject to constant interpretation and reinterpretation by individual and collective actors, which points once again to the close relationship, and even the possible interdependence (Padamsee 2009), of ideational and institutional factors.

Closely intertwined in actual political and policy processes, these two explanatory factors are both historically constructed and the product of ongoing interactions among actors, but they differ in part because institutions are embedded rules and ideas are not, in and of themselves (Béland and Cox 2011b). When ideas become institutionalized as the enforced rules of the game, they start to shape human action in a different way, thus becoming a different type of explanation (Parsons 2007). Much of the politics of ideas in public policy is about transforming these ideas into embedded institutions, but not all ideas are successful enough to become institutionalized policies in which concrete and enforceable rules are embedded. Some ideas are more influential than others and, if powerful actors can popularize or even impose them, have a better chance of becoming institutions (Hansen and King 2001). Conversely, discarded policy institutions such as the death penalty within the European Union may survive within political debates as a policy idea that has lost its legal and institutional status but that specific individuals and collectives may still embrace and promote (on the death penalty, see Hood and Hoyle 2015).

The above discussion is rather abstract and may give the impression that ideational and institutional analysis is only concerned with purely abstract explanatory factors. This is not the case in part because, in order to study their explanatory role, both ideas and institutions must be broken down into smaller units of analysis. There are different types of ideas and institutions in the real world and scholars must draw a clear line between them before studying how they could interact under particular circumstances (Béland and Waddan 2015). This is why this Element features a discussion about concrete types of ideas and institutions and how they might relate to different social and political actors.

The study of institutions is widely used in comparative research, as policy scholars and social scientists have demonstrated how existing institutions shape the behaviour of the actors that formulate and promote key policy ideas (Hall 1989; Orenstein 2008). Importantly, institutional factors that influence these actors are not only formal political institutions such as electoral and party systems; they also comprise historically constructed policy legacies that create both opportunities and constraints for policy-makers (Lecours 2005; Skocpol 1992; for a critical perspective, see Amenta 1998). This points to the analysis of self-reinforcing and self-undermining policy feedback (Jacobs and Weaver 2015), which are associated with historical institutionalism.

3 Institutionalisms and Institutions

The starting point of the discussion about the role of institutions in policy stability and change is historical institutionalism (Fioretos, Falleti, and Sheingate 2016; Lecours 2005; Orloff 1993; Pierson 1994; Skocpol 1992; Steinmo, Thelen, and Longstreth 1992), one of the three main types of new institutionalism that crystalized in the 1980s and early 1990s (Campbell 2004; Hall and Taylor 1996; Schmidt 2008).[1] It is useful to discuss historical institutionalism alongside these two other main types of new institutionalism in order to understand what is unique about it. First, rational-choice institutionalism is grounded in an economic perspective according to which actors make choices in a constraining institutional and material environment. These constraints typically foster "evolutionary change" and "strategic equilibrium" (Campbell 2004, p. 11). A classic example of rational-choice institutionalism is the work of economist Douglas North (1990) on path dependence and institutional continuity, which had a direct influence on scholars from other disciplines, including sociology (Mahoney 2000) and political science (Pierson 2000; for a critique of path dependence, see Kay 2005). Second, organizational institutionalism, as its name suggests, focuses on the development of organizations over time. More specifically, the emphasis of organizational institutionalism is on how "taken-for-granted cognitive and normative structures constrain (and enable) actors" (Campbell 2004, p 11). An early and widely cited example of organizational institutionalism is "The iron cage revisited," an article by sociologists Paul DiMaggio and Walter Powell (1983) that shows how the emergence of organizational fields favours isomorphism, a process whereby organizations become increasingly similar as the actors populating them seek to increase the

---

[1] For a critical discussion stressing the ideational side of historical institutionalism, see Hay and Wincott 1998; for a broad overview of new institutionalism, see Peters 2011.

legitimacy of these organizations by making them fit well into their institutional environment.

In contrast, as the name implies, historical institutionalism is centred on the historical development of institutions.[2] Even when dealing with single-country case studies, an institution's historical development is typically studied from a comparative angle. Historical institutionalism has a strong temporal orientation, which is why, in addition to focusing on formal political institutions and their impact on individual and collective behaviour, it also stresses the need to understand existing policies as institutions that can shape future policy decisions through what is known as policy feedback (Béland 2010a; Pierson 1993). A well-known example of historical institutionalism is *Protecting Soldiers and Mothers* by US sociologist and political scientist Theda Skocpol (1992). The work looks at political institutions and feedback effects from existing policies, such as Civil War pensions, to explain the specific course of social policy development in the United States before the New Deal. Although her book focuses on the United States, Skocpol applies a comparative lens where US actors, institutions, and policy legacies are compared to the ones found in other industrial countries to shed light on so-called American exceptionalism.

While rational-choice institutionalism focuses on strategic behaviour and organizational institutionalism on cultural norms, "[h]istorical institutionalists are eclectic; they use both of these approaches to specify the relationship between institutions and action" (Hall and Taylor 1996, p. 940). This eclectic approach makes historical institutionalism a potential vehicle for ideational analysis because it leaves room for the recognition of both the agency of actors and the central role of cultural and social meanings associated with ideas. Simultaneously, historical institutionalism has a rich comparative component much less evident in the two other forms of institutionalism. Finally, and even more crucially, historical institutionalism is the purest form of institutionalism in the sense that it is centred primarily on institutional explanations, which is actually not the case for rational-choice or organizational institutionalism. As Parsons (2007) shows, rational-choice institutionalists typically make structural arguments, and organizational sociologists tend to emphasize ideational explanations.

The purest form of institutionalism – historical institutionalism – has potential for ideational analysis, something that will become clearer in the discussion

---

[2] In the United States, historical institutionalism is related to American Political Development (APD), which promotes systematic historical perspectives on US politics and institutions. Like historical institutionalism, APD leaves much room for the study of ideas and some of the authors discussed in this Element arguably belong to both historical institutionalism and APD. On these issues, and APD more generally, see Orren and Skowronek 2004.

that follows, which focuses on early historical institutionalism work that paid direct attention to the role of ideas in politics and public policy. The focus on this earlier scholarship should not hide the shift away from ideational analysis within some of the more recent historical institutionalist scholarship, which has taken a structural and rational-choice turn (Blyth, Helgadottir, and Kring 2016). This tendency may have led authors such as Mark Bevir and Jason Blakely (2018, p. 7) to assume misleadingly that historical institutionalism is necessarily grounded in a narrow form of "naturalism" incompatible with what they call the "interpretative turn," which is ideational in nature. One of the contributions of this Element is to show once again how historical institutionalism, when properly used and understood, is an appropriate vehicle for the study of ideas as they potentially interact with institutions (on this issue see also Campbell 2004; Schmidt 2011). Rooted in this basic intellectual project, the following sections outline the key institutional factors at the heart of historical institutionalism before showing how this approach can lead to ideational analyses to explore the interaction and the potential interdependence of ideational and institutional processes in the politics of public policy.

4 Political Institutions and Public Policy

One of historical institutionalism's central assumptions is that political institutions have a durable impact on the ways in which actors mobilize within the policy process. First, historical institutionalism recognizes that political institutions can shape key political actors in the first place. This is the case for electoral rules that preside over the development of political parties, as party systems vary greatly from jurisdiction to jurisdiction. In her book *Parting at the Crossroads*, devoted to the development of health care reform in post–World War II Canada and the United States, political scientist Antonia Maioni (1998) explains how differences in party systems can shape policy development. According to her, in contrast to the US party system centred almost exclusively on the opposition between Democrats and Republicans, Canadian parliamentary institutions allowed for the advent of influential socialist parties in the 1930s and 1940s. The emergence of these parties at both the provincial and the federal levels increased the pressure on the then dominant political parties, especially the Liberal Party, to support the expansion of universal health coverage through federal funding (Maioni 1998).

Beyond the discussion about political parties, Maioni's (1998) work stresses how political institutions shape federalism and other forms of territorial politics. Constitutional design is key here, as the distinction between unitary and federal states is crucial for the study of both politics and public policy (Pierson 1995).

Yet, in contrast to scholars who describe federalism as a simple "variable" (Greer, Béland, Lecours, and Dubin 2019), historical institutionalists also point to the fact that the nature and policy effects of federal institutions vary greatly from one federal country to the next (Benz and Broschek 2013; Obinger, Leibfried, and Castles 2005). For example, in her work on the development of conditional cash transfers in Argentina and Brazil, Tracy Fenwick (2015) shows how the constitutional design of the Brazilian federal system grants much political autonomy to municipalities, which makes it possible for the president to work with them to neutralize potential interference from state governors. In contrast, Fenwick (2015) suggests that municipalities' weaker constitutional and institutional status in Argentina works to increase governors' power, making it harder for the president to circumvent them and promote the development of conditional cash transfers across the country.

In addition to party systems and federalism, another factor on which institutionalist scholars have focused is the role of courts. This role is particularly obvious in the United States, where scholars such as William Forbath (1991) and Victoria Hattam (1993) explore how the central role of the Supreme Court in that country in the late nineteenth and early twentieth centuries impacted labour unions' political strategies and their relationship to the state. Because they faced so much opposition from the Supreme Court and other legal institutions, US labour unions emphasized collective bargaining and downplayed the need for political mobilization, which had a major impact on policy development during the Progressive Era (Skocpol 1992). In her book, Hattam (1993) combines an institutionalist perspective with close attention to the role of ideas, arguing that "labour visions" and institutional factors are closely related.

Party systems, federalism, and the role of courts are only three ways in which political institutions can shape the mobilization of various individual and collective actors. A number of historical institutionalist scholars use the concept of veto point to offer a more systematic look at how political actors and institutions interact closely to impact the policy process. This helps identify how institutional configurations may empower specific actors and allow them to prevent policy reform from being adopted in the first place (Bonoli 2001; Immergut 1992; Kay 1999).[3] For instance, Immergut explains how certain political institutions can help determine physicians' political power by creating particular veto points they might use to influence policy (Immergut 1992).

---

[3] The concept of a veto point is often associated with the concept of a veto player, which has a slightly different meaning, in part because it derives more from rational-choice theory than from historical institutionalism (Tsebelis 2002; for a recent critical discussion, see Ganghof 2017).

Drawing on this scholarship, Stephen Kay (1999, p. 406) illustrates the historical institutionalist take on the role of political institutions by arguing that they "shape (but do not determine) political conflict by providing interest groups with varying opportunities to veto policy." From this perspective, institutions create both constraints and opportunities for political actors involved in the policy process without eliminating their agency, which leads to a nondeterministic take on the influence of institutions.

It is important, however, to recognize that some proponents of historical institutionalism have adopted a purely deterministic approach to policy stability and change that is problematic at best. This is the case of the work by Sven Steinmo and Jon Watts (1995) on the lack of universal health insurance in the United States. The authors attribute this to the fragmentation of political power, an institutional characteristic that increases the influence of interest groups capable of mobilizing against progressive reforms. For the authors, who were writing not long after the defeat of President Clinton's Health Security initiative, "the United States does not have comprehensive national health insurance (NHI) because American political institutions are biased against this type of reform" (Steinmo and Watts 1995; for a critical discussion, see Hacker 1997, p. 173). This type of strict institutional determinism is at odds with recent institutionalist literature on policy stability and change that stresses the complexity, ambiguity, and multiple potential effects of institutions over time (Béland and Waddan 2012; Mahoney and Thelen 2009; Palier 2005; Streeck and Thelen 2005). This understanding of institutions is also present in the recent literature on policy feedback, discussed in the next section.

5 Policy Feedback

Policy feedback is a key concept within the historical institutionalist tradition (Béland 2010a). Stressing the importance of this concept is essential in part because much of the literature focusing on the relationship between ideas and institutions simply neglects policy feedback at the expense of formal political institutions (Campbell 2004; Hay 2011; Schmidt 2011). Yet, feedback effects from existing policies can be as important as formal political institutions in accounting for policy stability and change over time (Béland 2010a; Pierson 1993).

Anticipated in the work of scholars such as Hugh Heclo (1974), Theodore J. Lowi (1964), and E. E. Schattschneider (1935), the concept of policy feedback is strongly associated with the historical institutionalist tradition from which it emerged. Simultaneously, this concept has been widely used since the late 1980s, both within and outside historical institutionalism, as a growing number of scholars have applied the concept to study policy stability and change (for overviews of the policy feedback literature, see Béland 2010a; Mettler and SoRelle 2018; Pierson 1993). At a general level, "[the] concept of policy feedback refers to this impact of previously enacted policies on future political behavior and policy choices. In other words, policy feedback is a temporal concept that points to the fact that over time, policy can shape politics" (Béland 2010a, p. 570), a point made explicitly by Lowi (1964) more than 50 years ago. Yet, just as political institutions can be broken down into different categories, policy feedback can take many different forms. To illustrate what policy feedback is, we can review three types of policy feedback: fostering interest-group mobilization, influencing the perceptions and behaviour of citizens, and creating "lock-in effects" that make future reforms harder to undertake.

First, the creation and development of public policies can shape interest-group mobilization over time (Pierson 1993, pp. 598–605). For instance, in her book *Protecting Soldiers and Mothers*, Skocpol (1992, p. 59) shows that the expansion of Civil War pensions led to the advent of large veteran organizations that fought to gain more comprehensive pension benefits for their members. This example suggests that, as policies develop over time, they help generate interest-group networks that are likely to fight for the expansion or, at least, the preservation of these policies during periods of retrenchment and restructuring. More recently, the case of Social Security reform in the United States during the Reagan years suggests that the emergence of large interest groups after the expansion of the program after 1945, such as the American Association of Retired Persons (AARP), increased pressure on the Republican president to preserve the program by striking a deal with Democrats in Congress (Béland 2007a; Light 1995; Pierson 1994).

Second, the development of public policy over time may affect the behaviour and perceptions of voters and citizens. In *How Policies Make Citizens*, for instance, Andrea Campbell (2003) suggests that the gradual expansion of US Social Security after World War II came to shape the perceptions and political behaviours of older citizens in the United States, notably by increasing their electoral participation and by lessening the participation gap between poorer and better-off elderly voters. This is the case because the very existence of this large federal social program motivated older people – especially the poorest among them who especially depend on public provision – to get involved in politics and pressure the White House and members of Congress to preserve *their* benefits (Campbell 2003).

Third, existing policies may generate "lock-in effects" over time. As Pierson wrote (1993, p. 608) in an early, seminal review essay on policy feedback, "Policies may create incentives that encourage the emergence of elaborate social and economic networks, greatly increasing the cost of adopting once-possible alternatives and inhibiting exit from a current policy path." The idea here is that existing policies that create strong lock-in effects are likely to reproduce over time in a path-dependent fashion, according to which the scope of change remains incremental in nature. This is the case because elected officials are likely to find the fiscal and political costs of moving away from these policies too high. Once again, old-age pensions illustrate this institutional logic as programs grounded in long-term fiscal arrangements are particularly hard to dismantle, in part because of the need to pay for current beneficiaries while transitioning towards a different system covering younger workers (Myles and Pierson 2001).

These three examples of policy feedback overlap and illustrate only a few of the many ways in which existing policy legacies can shape the politics of public policy. Over the last fifteen years, the concept of policy feedback has gained so much popularity that it has been used on its own outside of the broader historical institutionalist framework, primarily to focus on the effects of existing policies on public opinion (Campbell 2012; Mettler and SoRelle 2018). Although the literature on policy feedback originates from the United States, a growing number of scholars from other parts of the world, especially Europe, have also used the concept (e.g. Garritzmann 2015; Svallfors 2010).

This broader literature, as well as the three above examples, point to a tendency within the policy feedback literature to emphasize self-reinforcing effects associated with institutional continuity and path dependence at the expense of self-undermining phenomena, according to which existing policies may weaken their own support over time and create favourable conditions for their demise or, at least, their profound transformation (Jacobs and Weaver 2015; Weaver 2010). Following the recent trend in historical institutionalism to emphasize the potential for transformative change rather than to focus primarily on policy stability (Hacker 2004; Mahoney and Thelen 2009; Streeck and Thelen 2005; Thelen 2004), Alan Jacobs and Kent Weaver (2015) invite students of policy feedback to pay more attention to self-undermining feedback affects and the ways in which they can bring about transformative policy change. For Jacobs and Weaver (2015, p. 442), self-undermining policy feedback draws attention to "*endogenous* forces – processes deriving from policy itself – that frequently generate strong pressures, and expand the political opportunities, for policy change." What this means is simply that policies do not always become stronger over time and that factors internal to these policies may in part explain why they can gradually become more vulnerable to political attacks. In their article, Jacobs and Weaver (2015) use the example of the US health care system before the enactment of Obamacare in 2010, which generated its own problems and weaknesses in a way that gave ammunition to political actors seeking to transform it. More generally, their analysis identified three main types of self-undermining feedback that explain why certain policies become politically weaker rather than stronger over time: "the emergence of *unanticipated policy losses* for mobilized social interests, *cognitive* processes arising from interactions between strategic elites and loss-averse voters, and expansions in the *menu of available policy alternatives*" (Jacobs and Weaver 2015, p. 442). Stressing the importance of political actors and the ways in which they react to self-undermining feedback, their framework suggests that this concept is helpful in studying policy change and, more specifically, why certain policies lose rather than gain political support as the years and decades pass by.

From this perspective, a key aspect of policy feedback is that this historical institutionalist concept has a clear ideational component, which Jacobs and Weaver (2015, p. 442) allude to in the above quote when they refer to "*cognitive* processes." This recognition of the ideational side of policy feedback is not restricted to self-undermining processes; Pierson (1993, p. 626) stresses the "interpretative" side of policy feedback in his early review essay that focuses on self-reinforcing effects (see also Lynch, 2006: 199). This early ideational focus is a result of Heclo's (1974) emphasis on policy learning, which informed much of the early policy feedback literature (for a recent overview of the policy learning literature, see Dunlop and Radaelli 2018). When actors draw lessons from existing policies, the institutional characteristics of these policies and the ideas and assumptions of the experts, state bureaucrats, and elected officials who assess them mesh in ways that illustrate the relationship between ideas and institutions in policy development. The work of Peter Hall (1993) on policy learning and paradigm shifts illustrates the close connection between ideas and institutions in the early historical institutionalist literature. Unfortunately, too many contemporary students of policy feedback do not systematically explore this connection, a situation related in part to the above-mentioned push towards structural and rational-choice explanations within historical institutionalism (Blyth, Helgadottir, and Kring 2016). These critical remarks lead us to the next section focusing on how historical institutionalism, and institutionalism more generally, have paved the way to ideational analysis, which is a good way to remind today's institutionalist scholars that ideational analysis is potentially fertile ground for them (Blyth, Helgadottir, and Kring 2016; Campbell 2004; Schmidt 2008).

6 From Historical Institutionalism to Ideational Analysis

It is common to associate institutionalism with the role of ideas simply because many institutionalist scholars have explicitly studied the role of ideas, something that authors such as Blyth (2002), Campbell (2004), Hay (2006), and Schmidt (2008) have noted. Yet, in their work, historical institutionalists do not always focus on the role of ideas. For instance, scholars such as Paul Pierson (2000) have borrowed from rational-choice theory rather than from ideational analysis to explain institutional stability and change (on this point, see Hay 2006). In fact, attention to ideas within historical institutionalism seems to have declined since the early-mid-1990s (Blyth, Helgadottir, and Kring 2016). This is in part why this Element engages so directly with the early historical institutional scholarship: because it is more conducive to ideational analysis than some of its recent iterations, which are much more prone to engaging with structural arguments than with ideational ones (Blyth, Helgadottir, and Kring 2016).

Students of ideas react against these trends and advocate paying more attention to ideas within historical institutionalism (e.g., Béland and Hacker 2004; Blyth, Helgadottir, and Kring 2016; Merrien 1997; Peters, Pierre, and King 2005). This push is hardly surprising because the early work of key historical institutionalist researchers turns explicitly to the role of ideas. This suggests once again that, as originally conceived, historical institutionalism is an excellent potential vehicle for ideational analysis and, more important for this Element, an appropriate starting point for approaches seeking to combine ideational and institutional analysis.

Within historical institutionalism, the early work of Peter Hall (1986, 1989, 1993) has done a lot to advance ideational analysis. A specialist of economic policy, Hall has explicitly explored the role of economic ideas in their institutional context. This is clear in the introduction to his edited volume, *The Political Power of Economic Ideas*, which looks at the diffusion of Keynesian ideas across different advanced industrial countries. Drawing explicitly on the emerging historical institutionalist literature, Hall (1989, pp. 10–12) acknowledges the impact of state institutions and bureaucratic capacity on the politics of economic ideas. Although he recognizes that this approach is not the only possible perspective on economic ideas, he sets the scene for an institutionalist analysis of economic ideas that Margaret Weir (1989) takes on in her contribution to the volume. In that chapter, Weir (1989) stresses the role of state institutions and policy legacies in explaining why Keynesian ideas had a different policy impact in Britain than in the United States in the mid-twentieth century. In her book *Politics and Jobs*, Weir further explores the relationship between ideas and political institutions through an analysis of US employment policy. According to Weir (1992, pp. 19–20), "Two features of American political institutions have influenced the range of ideas that have been considered in national policymaking about employment. The first is the relative openness of the federal government to new ideas; the second is the limited capacity of the government to serve as a site for the production of ideas about employment." These remarks anticipate the institutionalist concept of a "knowledge regime" developed two decades later by John L. Campbell and Ove K. Pedersen (2011, 2014), which is discussed in Section 13

Beyond economic ideas and expertise, historical institutionalist scholars have explored how ideational and institutional factors interact to shape other policy areas. A striking example of this is the work of Robert C. Lieberman (2002, p. 700) on the politics of race in the United States. What his detailed empirical analysis suggests is that policy scholars study the "intersection of ideas and institutions" because "any fully convincing theory of political or institutional change must incorporate both [ideas and institutions] as constituent elements with reasonably equal weights." This claim that the politics of public policy should be understood at the "intersection of ideas and institutions" requires systematic attention.

As Lieberman (2002, p. 708) concludes,

> public policies are most fruitfully understood as the results of political conflicts in which particular elements of national cultural and ideological repertoires are mobilized and enacted into policy. These political struggles take place within historical and institutional contexts that define the allocation and exercise of political power and so shape policymaking, especially by constraining political behaviour through the operation of rules, norms, and organizational settings.

This quote points to an ideational reading of historical institutionalism that takes ideas seriously while exploring how they interact with institutional factors to impact policy actors' behaviours and decisions.

This discussion about ideational analysis within historical institutionalism leads us to address the difference between this type of scholarship, which is at the core of this Element, and discursive institutionalism, an approach put forward by Vivien Schmidt that focuses primarily on how different types of political discourses associated with particular institutional settings can shape policy change (2008, 2011). Instead of presenting her approach as an extension of historical institutionalism, Schmidt (2008, 2011) claims discursive institutionalism is a fourth type of institutionalism that both builds on and transcends organizational, rational choice, and historical institutionalism.

In contrast to historical institutionalism, however, discursive institutionalism focuses more on the impact of discourse as a causal force than on the impact of political institutions, which shape only the type of discourse actors use rather than their actual decisions. The starting point for discursive institutionalism is that discourse and ideas alone shape policy change, which means that political institutions simply determine why actors mobilize one type of discourse over the next, as is evident in Schmidt's (2002a) empirical work on welfare state adjustment. There, she suggests that single-actor institutional systems such as the United Kingdom rely on "communicative discourse" aimed at convincing the public to support reform rather than relying on "coordinative discourse," which is dominant in multi-actor institutional systems such as Germany, where political actors try to convince social partners such as business and union organizations to embrace reform (Schmidt 2002a). The distinction between these two types of discourse so central to discursive institutionalism (Schmidt 2008, 2011) suggests that, within that framework, institutions generally determine the type of discourse used rather than having a direct impact on policy decisions themselves, which are the product of ideational processes. In other words, the explanatory crux of discursive institutionalism is primarily ideational in nature.

As both Parsons (2007) and Jeremy Rayner (2015) suggest, the term "institutionalism" should be used when institutions are key causal factors that directly shape policy and political change, which is not the case with discursive institutionalism (Schmidt 2008), which is a potentially confusing label, at least from an explanatory standpoint. In contrast, following Lieberman (2002) and other historical institutionalists who pay close attention to ideational processes, this Element assumes that both ideas and institutions can directly shape policy stability and change, and that determining how the two might interact and even become interdependent to produce political and policy effects is an empirical question that raises crucial analytical issues, which are discussed in the remainder of this Element. Before exploring these issues, and to provide a counterpoint to the earlier discussion about political institutions and policy feedback, the next section further discusses what ideas are and how they can shape policy stability and change. Once they know more about how different types of ideas matter (Jacobs 2009; Mehta 2011), readers will be in a much better position to discuss how they might interact with institutions.

7 Mapping Ideas: Policy Paradigms and Beyond

As Parsons (2007) claims, ideational processes constitute a particular type of explanation in political and policy research. In Section 2 I broadly defined ideas as actors' historically constructed beliefs and perceptions.[4] Yet there are

---

[4] The literature on the role of ideas has expanded dramatically over the last two decades and many theoretical and empirical discussions about their nature and impact are available. For example: Ban, 2016; Béland and Cox 2011a; Berman 1998, 2013; Bhatia and Coleman 2003; Bleich 2003; Bradford 1998; Blyth 2002; Campbell 2002; Gofas and Hay 2009; Hansen and King 2001; Jacobs 2009, 2011; McNamara 1998; Palier and Surel 2005; Parsons 2002; Schmidt 2002b; Walsh 2000;

different types of ideas, and mapping them is crucial because, like institutions, they constitute a general category that can be broken down into different subcategories. This task makes it easier for scholars to study how particular types of ideas might intersect with different types of institutions, such as federalism, party systems, or policy legacies (Béland and Waddan 2015). Although it is not appropriate to cover all possible types of ideas in this manuscript, discussing at least some of them should give the reader an idea of the sheer diversity of the ideational processes policy researchers can explore in their empirical work. In the literature, specific types of ideas are often studied independently from one another, which can create empirical blind spots and, more importantly, a lack of systematic discussion about the ideational explanatory logic. The advantage of discussing different types of ideas together is that it helps us to understand what ideational processes are at the most general explanatory level, while also revealing their sheer empirical diversity and the different ways in which they can be studied.

Another important reason why discussing different types of ideas together is useful is that scholars may not want to focus exclusively on the popular and useful concept of policy paradigm, which is only one of the core concepts used in the ideational literature. Drawing on the work of Jane Jenson (1989) on "societal paradigms," Peter Hall (1993), who popularized the concept of policy paradigm, points to the articulation of particular goals with policy problems and instruments. Considering this, policy paradigms are much more complex than stand-alone problem definitions and policy solutions, as they articulate these with broader policy goals. Hall (1993) claims that paradigm shifts are a transformative form of policy change that involves more than a change in policy settings (first order change) or in policy instruments (second order change). This is the case because paradigm shifts feature a change in settings, instruments, and broader policy goals all at once, which Hall (1993) refers to as third order change. Since the publication of Hall's seminal 1993 *Comparative Politics* article on the topic, the concept of policy paradigm has generated a broad critical literature that stresses the importance of ideas in both policy stability and change (e.g. Carstensen 2011; Coleman, Skogstad, and Atkinson 1996; Daigneault 2014; Hogan and Howlett 2015; Skogstad 2011).

Discussing a couple of existing ideational typologies is an appropriate way to begin mapping the sheer diversity of ideational processes beyond the exclusive focus on policy paradigms mentioned earlier. First, in his chapter in *Ideas and Politics in Social Science Research*, Jal Mehta (2011) offers a tripartite typology

---

White 2002. The "ideational turn" (Blyth 1997) occurred simultaneously with the emergence of related scholarship about discursive (Hajer 1995) and interpretative (Bevir and Rhodes 2003) processes in governance and public policy.

of ideas inspired by the work of John W. Kingdon (2011). For Mehta (2011), there are three main types of ideas within the policy process: problem definitions, policy solutions, and public philosophies or zeitgeist. The first two types are relatively straightforward and widely studied within the policy literature. First, how policy problems are defined is a key aspect of the policy process and has long been a field of research in its own right (on problem definition, see Gusfield 1980; Rochefort and Cobb 1994; Stone 2012).[5] While the ideational nature of problem definition is undeniable, problem definition should be discussed within a broader ideational context instead of as a stand-alone concept, a problem that Mehta (2011) avoids by including problem definition in his ideational typology. Second, policy solutions are concrete ideas that actors debate within the policy process (Mehta 2011). These solutions are typically formulated by experts and bureaucrats within what Kingdon (2011) calls the policy stream. These solutions, which he labels policy alternatives, are not developed simply as responses to emerging policy problems. Instead, pre-existing solutions can be coupled with new and emerging problems in what amounts to policy recycling and adaptation (Kingdon 2011). The struggle over policy solutions is a central part of the policy process as different actors promote their favourite type of policy solution, which often takes the form of a generic policy instrument. For instance, proponents of privatization as a policy instrument are well organized and tend to promote their preferred type of policy solution regardless of the policy problem currently on the agenda. These supply-side actors are in the business of diffusing particular types of policy solutions and are known as "instrument constituencies" (Béland and Howlett 2016; Voss and Simons 2014).

Studying problem definitions and policy solutions does not pose any major analytical challenges. This is not the case with the much broader public philosophies and zeitgeist that Mehta includes as the last element of his three-fold ideational typology. For Mehta (2011, p. 40), a public philosophy is "a view, often voiced by political parties[,] about the appropriate role of government given certain assumptions about the market and society, whereas the zeitgeist is a disparate set of cultural, social, or economic assumptions that are overwhelmingly dominant in public discourse at a given moment in time." The concept of public philosophy is closely related to that of political ideology,

---

[5] For something to become a policy problem, individuals must typically understand how the issues they face are collective in nature and worthy of collective action and state intervention, processes related to what C. Wright Mills (1959) calls "sociological imagination." In addition to "sociological imagination," another potentially helpful concept for the critical study of problem definition is "problematization," which was formulated by Michel Foucault (1997) and later developed by Carol Bacchi (2012).

which has been successfully articulated and studied by scholars such as Michael Freeden (1996, 2003) and Sheri Berman (2006, 2011).[6] Studying political ideologies such as liberalism and socialism is a fruitful way to look at the politics of ideas policy at a broader and more abstract level, complementing the analysis of the narrower problem definitions and policy solutions Mehta (2011) discusses. As for the concept of zeitgeist, it poses some clear epistemological challenges because it points to vague, fragmented, and unconscious ideas that are challenging to study empirically (Béland and Cox 2011b, p. 14).

Second, another typology of ideas available in the literature is articulated by John L. Campbell (2004) in *Institutional Change and Globalization*. His typology features four kinds of ideas. The first two – policy paradigms and public sentiments – are located in the background of the policy process, while the other two – programs and frames – are located in the foreground. Like many other scholars, Campbell (2004) discusses policy paradigms in reference to the work of Hall (1993), which is summarized above.

As for public sentiments, they are more diffuse than policy paradigms but more concrete than Mehta's zeitgeist. This is the case because public sentiments are public perceptions of the general population and can be measured in part by using polling techniques. At the same time, public sentiments are not only about public opinion in the narrow sense of the term; they can also point to relatively stable cultural categories and understandings (Dobbin 1994; Pfau-Effinger 2005; Steensland 2008). Even more than policy paradigms, these cultural categories and understandings are clearly located in the background of the policy process.

Conversely, Campbell (2004) locates programs and frames in the foreground of the policy process. First, programs constitute "road maps" (Goldstein and Keohane 1993) that help policy-makers "chart a clear and specific course of action" (Campbell 2004, p. 94). Policy and party platforms are concrete examples of programs that scholars can study to better understand policy-makers' objectives and strategies. Programs differ from paradigms in part because they are less technical in nature, and in part because they are meant to articulate a prominent political discourse about public policy.

Second, frames are "symbols and concepts" (Campbell 2004, p. 94) that policy actors mobilize to justify and promote their policy proposals and convince the public and key interest groups to support them.[7] There are clear similarities between the concept of frame and the concept of discourse Schmidt (2002a,

---

[6] For more information on political ideologies, see Freeden, Sargent, and Stears 2013.

[7] For a different take on the concept of frames, which originates in part in the work of sociologist Erving Goffman (1974), see Schön and Rein 1994. The analysis of framing processes has long been central to social movement research (Benford and Snow 2000).

2008) uses. Another related concept is that of narrative, according to which policy and political actors tell stories about the world to affect public perceptions and legitimize specific problem definitions and policy proposals (Somers and Block 2005; Stone 2012). Just like discourse and narratives, frames are largely strategic in nature and typically draw on existing ideological and cultural repertoires to justify the policies they support and to delegitimize the policies they actively oppose. Frames are used in policy battles that are dialogical in nature in the sense that actors respond to their opponents by putting forward alternative frames to attack them and weaken support for their policy solutions (Béland 2005; on dialogism, see Bakhtin 1981). This point is similar to Schmidt's (2011, p. 56) claim that discourse constitutes an "interactive process" that involves communication on the part of political actors who seek to persuade others to support their policy solutions and join their coalition.

The above discussion about frames, discourse, and narratives suggests that researchers frequently use different concepts to refer to similar ideational processes (Béland 2016a). These conceptual and terminological boundaries are largely artificial and prevent scholars interested in a particular type of idea from engaging with the work of other academics who use different terms to talk about very similar things. Being aware of the broader ideational literature and the diversity of the terms and concepts available within it is essential because it allows researchers to break artificial boundaries created by a scholar's attachment to particular terminologies and keywords, which makes it harder for scholars to create extended and fruitful dialogues about the role of ideas in public policy. The next section continues the exploration of the role of ideas in the politics of public policy through a discussion of their role across the different moments of the policy cycle, which is just another way of mapping their potential influence.

8 Ideas, Actors, and the Policy Cycle

Scholars have long divided the policy cycle into different moments (Howlett, Ramesh, and Perl 2009). These moments may vary in number, but they typically include agenda-setting, formulation, decision-making, implementation, and evaluation. These moments do not always follow a strict order and the boundaries between them are sometimes fuzzy (Howlett, Ramesh, and Perl 2009). Despite its limitations, the policy cycle approach allows us to break down the policy process into distinct moments and to explore the role of ideas and of the actors carrying them within each of such moments.

First, during the agenda-setting moment, actors such as experts and journalists define certain problems and push them in and out of the policy agenda (on agenda-setting, see Baumgartner and Jones 1993; Green-Pedersen and Walgrave 2014; Kingdon 2011; Soroka 2002). Thus, within the policy cycle, the issue of problem definition discussed earlier plays an especially central role during the agenda-setting moment (Howlett, Ramesh, and Perl 2009). Yet agenda-setting is not only about how problems are defined and understood. Agenda-setting involves competition for attention among different actors and the problems they hope to move onto the policy agenda. This "politics of attention" (Jones and Baumgartner 2005) is crucial across different policy areas because the number of issues policy-makers can consider at one point in time is necessarily limited (Kingdon 2011). Drawing attention to particular problems is largely a discursive and ideational process where actors seek to depict specific social problems as both pressing and requiring state intervention through the creation of new policies or the expansion of existing measures.

The second moment, policy formulation, also features the role of ideas prominently. This is the case because designing policy solutions to address economic and social problems often involves explicit competition among particular ideas and proposals (Kingdon 2011; Mehta 2011). Policy formulation involves the mobilization of numerous actors ranging from academics and consultants to think tanks and international organizations. As they get involved in policy design – a strategic, goal-oriented activity (Howlett and Mukherjee 2014) – these actors may draw on concrete policy paradigms to make sense of currently available policy proposals (Daigneault 2014; Hall 1993), or even participate in a specific instrument constituency associated with their preferred solutions (Béland and Howlett 2016; Voss and Simons 2014).

Third, during the decision-making moment, elected officials, policy entrepreneurs (Kingdon 2011), and advocacy coalitions (Sabatier 1988) fight over the enactment of concrete policy solutions. Here, framing processes become particularly relevant for the "construction of the need to reform" (Cox 2001) and for bringing the general public and key constituencies on board (Bhatia and Coleman 2003; Schmidt 2002a). Framing battles over social policy are likely to involve broader political ideologies (Berman 2011; Freeden 2003) and draw on existing cultural categories (Steensland 2008) and public sentiments (Campbell 2004). The analysis of decision-making can take ideas in the foreground of policy debates into account and, simultaneously, connect these ideas with ideational realities located in the background of these debates. This kind of analysis can help explain why policy entrepreneurs gather support to facilitate or prevent the enactment of major reforms but also, more generally, how embedded beliefs located in the background of social policy debates may enable or stand in the way of change (Steensland 2008).

Implementation, the fourth moment, is probably the most neglected of the policy cycle as far as ideational research is concerned. This is a shame because implementation is a crucial aspect of policy development and has received direct attention from policy scholars (e.g., Bardach 1977; Lipsky 2010; Pressman, and Wildavsky 1984; for an overview, see Béland and Ridde 2016). The policy implementation literature suggests that what happens to a program after its legislative adoption is crucial in determining its success or failure on the ground. For instance, street-level bureaucrats (Lipsky 2010) can reshape policies as they implement them. At the same time, particular constituencies, such as labour unions and professional organizations, can sometimes shape the implementation of a policy. Ideas can play a direct role in implementation processes – for instance, when the embedded beliefs of policy experts and street-level bureaucrats are at odds with new reforms. When this happens, these actors can oppose reforms on the ground in a way that is detrimental to their effective implementation (Béland and Ridde 2016).

Finally, in contrast to implementation, evaluation is a moment of the policy process that easily lends itself to ideational analysis as it relates to popular ideational concepts such as policy transfer (Dolowitz and Marsh 2000), lesson drawing (Rose 1991), and social learning (Bennett and Howlett 1992; Hall 1993; Heclo 1974). Although policy evaluation can take the form of rigorous analysis informed by empirical evidence, ideological biases, as well as contested interpretations of existing policy legacies and what constitutes proper evidence, are likely to emerge during the evaluation process, especially when this process relates directly to ongoing political debates. Moreover, experts and government officials may debate what counts as proper evidence on which policy decisions could be based (on the politics of evidence, see Parkhurst 2017). Finally, the extent to which civil servants and other policy actors absorb academic knowledge and evidence to inform their decisions varies greatly based on factors such as the level of education of these actors (Ouimet et al. 2009).

In this context, it is not surprising that policy learning and evaluation are central to the literature on paradigms, according to which the lessons drawn from existing policies are shaped by the assumptions of the actors drawing these lessons (Hall 1993). In a more general way, policy learning is not a purely objective endeavour but a political reality that is not without ideological struggles (Fischer 2003). As the above discussion suggests, such struggles are not just about policy evaluation and are ever-present across the policy cycle, where they interact with institutional processes. To think more systematically about how ideational and institutional processes interact among themselves and with political actors, the next section discusses existing theories of the policy process.

9 Reconsidering Theories of the Policy Process: Ideas, Institutions, and Actors

Existing theories of the policy process have made a tremendous contribution to the study of public policy (Weible and Sabatier 2018).[8] Yet, they generally suffer from a number of limitations as far as an analysis of the interaction between ideas and institutions is concerned. Considering the diversity of these theories, the following critical discussion focuses mainly on two particularly prominent theories of the policy process: the multiple-streams framework (Kingdon 2011) and the advocacy coalition framework (Sabatier 1988). Before discussing the added value of these two popular approaches, I will outline the most significant limitations of the existing theories of the policy process more generally.

First, theories of the policy process are not always as clear as they should be about their own explanatory logics, which makes it harder for scholars to assess their relative causal merits (Lindquist and Wellstead 2018). Second, and more specifically, although most existing theories of the policy process acknowledge the role of ideational processes in one way or another, they do not necessarily define them as key explanatory factors. For instance, while the advocacy coalition framework focuses on policy learning and the core beliefs of the actors who form advocacy coalitions, these ideational processes are not typically credited with producing transformative policy changes, which are generally theorized as the outcome of exogenous shocks (Fischer 2003, p. 99). As for the multiple-streams framework, it deals explicitly with the role of ideas, but its theorization of ideational processes remains rather vague and narrow from an explanatory perspective (Béland 2016b). These critical remarks should not hide the fact that these two theories of the policy process certainly do contribute to the study of ideas in public policy. The same remark applies to at least two other theories – the narrative policy framework (Shanahan et al. 2018) and punctuated equilibrium theory (Baumgartner, Jones, and Mortensen 2018) – that both explicitly emphasize the role of ideational processes and make a direct contribution to the study of ideas in public policy. This is especially the case for punctuated equilibrium theory, which did a lot early on to draw the attention of policy scholars to ideational constructs such as "policy images" and "policy monopolies" (Baumgartner and Jones 1993; see also Jones and Baumgartner 2005). A limitation of both punctuated equilibrium theory and the narrative

---

[8] These theories are summarized and critically discussed in Weible and Sabatier (2018).

policy framework concerns their focus on a small range of ideational processes and their excessively limited attention to how they interact with institutional processes to explain the politics of public policy.

The third limitation, with a couple of exceptions, is that existing theories of the policy process pay relatively limited attention to the impact of political institutions and policy legacies, seriously undermining their potential for comparative policy analysis.[9] Here, the advocacy coalition framework, which does pay some attention to political institutions (Jenkins-Smith et al. 2018; Sabatier 1988), fares better than the multiple-streams framework, which is largely silent about the role of institutions within the policy process (Béland 2016b; Zohlnhöfer, Herweg, and Huß 2016; Weir 1992). Fourth, at least in their traditional forms, theories of the policy process, including the advocacy coalition framework and the multiple-streams framework, pay limited attention to transnational actors and processes and how these interact with domestic actors and institutions.

Despite their limitations, existing theories of the policy process, and especially the advocacy coalition framework and the multiple-streams framework, can help identify some of the key actors involved in the politics of public policy (Béland and Howlett 2016). Discussing these actors is necessary to make the study of ideas more concrete and to move away from the claim that ideational analysis is "idealistic" in nature and detached from people and processes (Béland and Cox 2011b).

First, the concept of the advocacy coalition as formulated by Sabatier (1988) is an excellent example of a collective policy actor that gathers around specific ideational processes: in this case, core beliefs that unite actors. As Sabatier (1988, p. 133) puts it, advocacy coalitions are "composed of people from various organizations who share a set of normative and causal beliefs and who often act in concert. At any particular point in time, each coalition adopts a strategy(s) envisaging one or more institutional innovations which it feels will further its policy objectives." Advocacy coalitions exist across different policy areas and their existence has been well documented (Schlager 1995; Weible et al. 2011). Despite its excessive emphasis on ideational stability (Carstensen 2010), the concept of an advocacy coalition points to the ways in

---

[9] I would like to thank Grace Skogstad for her insights about this issue. Out of the seven theories outlined in the latest edition of the Weible and Sabatier (2018) volume, only policy feedback theory (Mettler and SoRelle 2018) and the institutional analysis framework (Schlager and Cox 2018) are centred on institutional processes. This is hardly surprising because policy feedback is a concept that emerged within historical institutionalism, and because the institutional analysis framework is based on the work of rational-choice institutionalist Elinor Ostrom (1990), whose contribution to the study of politics of public policy beyond environmental issues remains relatively limited in scope.

which ideational processes play a role in coalition building, which is explored further in Section 12.

Second, the concept of policy entrepreneurs associated with the multiple-streams framework and coined by Kingdon (2011) illustrates another way in which turning to concrete actors is necessary to grasp the multifaceted role of ideas in the politics of public policy. For Kingdon (2011, p. 122), policy entrepreneurs are simply "advocates for [policy] proposals or for the prominence of an idea." Policy entrepreneurs can help bring about change by promoting specific policy alternatives and by linking them to problems that move onto the agenda. This is why policy entrepreneurs (e.g., individual experts, think tanks, or political parties) are central figures in the politics of ideas (Béland 2016b; Mehta 2011; Roberts and King 1991). Beyond the work of Kingdon (2011), there is also a large literature on the relationship between policy entrepreneurs and policy change, which has a significant ideational component (Mintrom and Norman 2009; Mintrom and Luetjens 2017).

Advocacy coalitions and policy entrepreneurs are key actors that scholars interested in the role of ideas in public policy ignore at their own peril. Yet, as Kingdon (2011, p. 72) himself claims, "nobody has a monopoly on ideas. They come from a plethora of different sources." This claim points to the plurality of actors involved in the politics of ideas. Just as ideational processes come in different forms and shapes, so do the actors that articulate, promote, or resist them. As John Campbell (2004, p. 101) points out, specific categories of actors are generally associated with particular types of ideas. Returning to the four types of ideas discussed above, he suggests that programs are mainly the realm of politicians and civil servants, that paradigms are primarily the business of experts and academics, that frames are produced in large part by spin doctors and political advisors, and that public sentiments are mainly about ordinary citizens and other constituents, who are the "targets of framers" (Campbell 2004, p. 104). To this list, Campbell (2004) adds brokers, who link these different actors and types of ideas to help bring about policy change. Under specific circumstances, consultants, political parties, business organizations, labour unions, and think tanks can become key ideational brokers involved in the politics of policy change (Campbell 2004, pp. 104–107). Brokers have much in common with policy entrepreneurs (Kingdon 2011). This remark suggests that students of ideational processes must pay close attention to individual and collective actors who might act as what French political scientists Bruno Jobert and Pierre Muller (1987) call "mediators" – i.e., as political actors who hold ideational authority within a specific policy area. The role of such mediators points once again to the need to pay close attention to policy actors and elites in the study of ideational processes (Genieys and Smyrl 2008). Simultaneously, this discussion relates to the need to combine the study of ideas with the analysis of political and policy leadership, something that Sabina Stiller (2010) has done in her book *Ideational Leadership in German Welfare State Reform.*

Although ideational leadership is a crucial issue that requires systematic attention, it should not hide the fact that institutional processes can also affect the development of policy actors and their ideas over time. To illustrate this reality further, the next section turns to transnational actors and how their impact on the diffusion of policy ideas around the world is mediated in large part by domestic political institutions.

10 Ideas, Political Institutions, and Transnational Actors

The role of transnational actors and processes is a key theoretical issue in contemporary policy research (e.g., Chwieroth 2010; Deacon 2007; Dolowitz and Marsh 2000; Mahon and McBride 2008; Noy 2017; Orenstein 2008; Skogstad 2011; Stone 2004; Tarrow 2005; Woods 2006). Direct attention to transnational actors and the ways in which they interact with domestic actors and institutions also improves comparative policy analysis, especially in contrast to existing theories on the policy process (Weible and Sabatier 2018) that typically pay limited attention to transnational actors and processes.

From the historical institutionalist perspective adopted in this Element, transnational actors can be understood as a potential source of ideational diffusion that, to exert policy influence in specific countries, must interact with domestic actors who are themselves shaped by national political institutions (Orenstein 2008). In other words, institutionally speaking, the main question here is how ideas, political institutions, and transnational actors interact to shape domestic policy decisions. This is an important question to tackle because much of the early historical institutionalist literature is silent about transnational actors, in part because its project originated largely in the broader intellectual project of *Bringing the State Back In* (Evans, Rueschemeyer, and Skocpol 1985). Yet, the ongoing debate on globalization has pushed a number of institutionalist scholars to explore how institutions affect, and are affected by, transnational actors involved in the domestic policy process (Béland 2009; Campbell 2004; Orenstein 2008)

Before addressing this issue, it is essential to define who these transnational actors are. Just like domestic policy actors, transnational actors take different forms. Among the main types of transnational actors, the most studied are probably international organizations such as the World Bank and the International Monetary Fund (IMF), who play a direct role in diffusing specific policy ideas all over the world (Chwieroth 2010; Noy 2017; Orenstein 2008; Woods 2006). These organizations, working with like-minded individuals and organizations, can act as transnational policy entrepreneurs to promote specific policy solutions within international key arenas and across many different countries (Orenstein 2008). Transnational policy entrepreneurs can also take the form of instrument constituencies, which are transnational networks of experts and organizations promoting a particular policy instrument and the concrete policy solutions attached to it (Béland and Howlett 2016; Voss and Simons 2014). Other transnational actors include international experts and consultants participating in what are known as epistemic communities, which gather academics and researchers working on specific policy issues (Haas 1992). These are only a few examples of transnational actors, all of which are eager and capable of diffusing policy ideas across different jurisdictions.

Individual and collective actors use various methods to diffuse their ideas around the world, including lobbying, networking, social media, official reports, and international conferences. Yet, if these actors want to influence domestic public policy, they have no choice but to interact with national and subnational social, political, and bureaucratic actors. This is the case because, as Mitchell Orenstein (2008) has shown in his book on pension privatization, international organizations such as the World Bank and other transnational actors do not have veto power over country-specific legislation, which requires them to work with domestic actors to get things done and make sure the policy ideas they promote internationally are both formally adopted and properly implemented in the countries they target. Even if coercion stemming from IMF and World Bank loans can force the hand of reluctant domestic actors, Orenstein (2008) suggests that financial pressure through conditionalities is not the only or even the main channel through which transnational actors influence domestic policy decisions. Ideational persuasion is a key form of transnational influence here, as transnational actors, who often form coalitions to coordinate their policy diffusion efforts, speak directly to domestic veto actors to convince them that it is in their best interests to enact particular policy solutions. For Orenstein (2008), political institutions are crucial here because they generally determine who has veto power within each country. This in turns orients the discursive and lobbying efforts of transnational actors, who generally target veto actors because their support is necessary for domestic policy change to take place.[10]

---

[10] It should be stressed, however, that transnational actors can work directly with civil society organizations such as labour unions, social movements, and professional associations that do not have any legislative or bureaucratic veto power in the hope that these organizations could pressure formal veto actors to deliver the policy decisions and outcomes transnational actors promote.

Shaping domestic veto actors is not the only way political institutions can have an impact on the transnational diffusion of policy ideas. For instance, as Schmidt (2002a, 2008) suggests, these institutions also determine what type of discourse is used to increase support for reform in specific countries, a situation that is likely to affect the framing strategies of transnational actors eager to influence domestic policy debates and promote their own ideas within them. At the same time, existing policy legacies shape the ways in which transnational policy ideas are adapted to each country. This is the case because these transnational ideas are typically *translated* to fit into existing domestic institutions and policy legacies (Campbell 2004). According to John Campbell (2004, p. 80), "translation involves the combination of *new* externally given elements received through diffusion as well as old locally given ones inherited from the past." This adaptation of external elements to national characteristics is not purely institutional in nature because it involves the reworking of cultural and symbolic elements through framing and discursive processes. For instance, new language can be introduced to make a foreign policy idea sound like a more obvious fit within existing domestic cultural and ideational repertoires.

This is what happened when the United States adopted social insurance at the federal level in the mid-1930s. Briefly, this European invention was framed as rooted in "American values" such as self-reliance. Thus, payroll contributions created "earned rights" and politically strong entitlements defined in sharp contrast with more politically vulnerable social assistance benefits, which became closely associated with the negative cultural category of dependency and the language of "welfare" (Fraser and Gordon 1994; Steensland 2008). At the same time, as already mentioned, the choice of social insurance as a way to finance federal old-age pensions was related to the limited fiscal capacity of the federal government, which made the payroll contributions associated with this policy instrument particularly attractive within existing domestic institutional and policy legacies (Béland 2007a; Leff 1983).

The above example suggests that transnational policy ideas such as social insurance are selected by domestic veto actors in part due to exiting institutional legacies before being translated to adapt to these legacies and to national cultural and ideological repertoires (Campbell 2004). More generally, this is an example of how ideational and institutional factors combine to facilitate policy diffusion through domestic decision-making and translation processes that shape the ways in which domestic and transnational realities intersect. This discussion leads us to explore how national and political identities evolve over time through similar and equally complex interactions among ideational and institutional processes.

11 Ideas, Institutions, and Identities

The concept of identity points to ideational processes embedded in the logic-of-interpretation as it relates to the way people see themselves (e.g., Béland 2017; Campbell 2004, p. 97; Hattam 1993; Jenson 1989; Wendt 1999). At the same time, identities are grounded in institutional norms and rules, which is clear in the work of James Fearon (1999, p. ii), who suggests that the concept of identity has two essential meanings today: "(a) a social category, defined by membership rules and (alleged) characteristic attributes or expected behaviors, or (b) socially distinguishing features that a person takes a special pride in or views as unchangeable but socially consequential (or (a) and (b) at once)." From an ideational and institutional perspective, identities are both institutionalized social categories and intersubjective meanings, which is another way to say that they have closely related institutional and ideational components (Béland 2017).

Both individual and collective identities can take different forms as they relate to issues ranging from age, gender, race, and ethnicity to nationality, profession, religion, and sexual orientation. For a long time, outside specific research areas such as gender and ethnic studies, the concept of identity did not feature prominently in mainstream academic policy debates; however, things are changing, especially as economists, who ignored identities for a long time, are finally turning to this concept traditionally associated with anthropology, psychology, sociology, and, to a lesser extent, political science (Akerlof and Kranton 2010). What George Akerlof and Rachel Kranton (2010) remind us in their book, *Identity Economics*, is that individual and collective identities, as they are embedded in concrete social norms, shape the attitudes and behaviours of economic, social, and political actors. This means that identity is an explanatory category present across society that institutionalist scholars should pay special attention to, as it points to the close connection between ideas and institutions through the constant making and remaking of collective norms and boundaries.

Ignoring identities in policy analysis in contemporary societies would create an enormous blind spot because the concept of identity is essential in explaining highly charged political struggles over crucial issues such as gender equality, immigration policy, nationalism, and secularism. This concept is also helpful in explaining political and policy processes that are explicitly about identities because identity formation is a key component of numerous forms of political and policy mobilizations, including social movements (Polletta and Jasper 2001) and political parties (Huddy and Bankert 2017). Moreover, support for a particular party or candidate can be rooted in specific racial identities. For example, in *Identity Crisis*, John Sides, Michael Tesler, and Lynn Vavreck (2018) show how racial and ethnic identities related to policy issues such as immigration explained in part the election of Donald Trump to the US presidency in November 2016. More generally, the politics of populism associated with President Trump is largely about the reframing of national identities as populist politicians define "the people" and their "enemy" in dichotomous terms that can increase support for exclusionary and illiberal policies (Müller 2016).

Beyond populism, the framing and reframing of national identities can directly affect the politics of redistribution, which can intersect with territorial institutions and policy legacies (Béland and Lecours 2008). For example, in Belgium, territorial identities have long shaped the politics of social security as it relates to both federal institutions and regional structural inequalities. In Belgium, Dutch-speaking Flanders is wealthier than French-speaking Wallonia. The territorially centralized nature of the country's social security system, which emerged decades before the gradual federalization of the country began in the early 1970s, has allowed Flemish nationalists seeking greater decentralization, and even outright independence, to frame Walloons as a fiscal burden for their region. Flemish nationalists claim that territorial redistribution towards their Walloon neighbours is illegitimate simply because they do not belong to the Flemish nation, which these nationalists describe as the only source of fiscal and economic solidarity. For them, Belgium is not a nation, so redistribution among the country's regions and language groups is simply illegitimate (Béland and Lecours 2008). This example suggests that identities can become key framing devices that influence political mobilization and shape ongoing debates about existing policy institutions as they intersect with structural forms of inequality – in this case, the economic gap between Flanders and Wallonia.

The relationship between structural inequality and identity as an ideational and institutional reality finds another expression in what Charles Tilly (1998, p. 6) labels "categorical inequalities." These inequalities are grounded in identity dichotomies (e.g., citizen and foreigner, male and female, and straight and gay) that help produce and reproduce these inequalities, which are themselves embedded in relatively stable ideational and institutional boundaries (Tilly 1998).[11] This is another example of how identities, as ideational and institutional hybrids that shape social and political boundaries, can affect key forms of inequality that intersect with policy issues such as economic redistribution and welfare state programming.

---

[11] On identity boundaries more generally as they relate to inequalities, see Bourdieu 1984; Lamont and Molnár 2002; Tilly 2005.

These boundaries have a direct meaning for public policy research as they draw our attention to the ways in which ideational categories such as identities are embedded in policy institutions through what Anne Schneider and Helen Ingram (1993) call the social construction of target populations.[12] The ideational categories that create boundaries around recipient populations are institutionalized through the eligibility criteria of public policies (Schneider and Ingram 1993). From this perspective, identity categories and boundaries are embedded in policy rules and legacies that allow for their reproduction over time. The ideational nature of these categories is straightforward because, as Schneider and Ingram (1993, p. 335) write,

> The social construction of a target population refers to (1) the recognition of the shared characteristics that distinguish a target population as socially meaningful, and (2) the attribution of specific, valence-oriented values, symbols, and images to the characteristics. Social constructions are stereotypes about particular groups of people that have been created by politics, culture, socialization, history, the media, literature, religion, and the like.

From this perspective, these social constructions are also cultural categories that can have a causal impact on key policy decisions (Steensland 2008) that reflect and reinforce structural inequalities and their cultural meanings as they become institutionally embedded in public policies. For example, the US debate on social assistance points to how gendered and racial categories became part of larger categories such as "welfare," symbolically contaminating beneficiaries of programs deemed inconsistent with dominant cultural norms. This situation can exacerbate the economic, social, and political disadvantages facing members of these categories. Yet, as Brian Steensland (2008) suggests, cultural categories such as "welfare" can have a causal impact on the policy process, which was the case in the US during the Nixon years (1969–1974), as "welfare" became such a controversial and problematic idea that it jeopardized federal social assistance reform.

In the United States, the stigmatization facing disadvantaged target populations, such as those on "welfare," typically contrasts with the higher cultural and social status of people who receive social insurance benefits (Campbell 2003; Fraser and Gordon 1994). These contrasting social constructions are crucial because they shape both public sentiments and reform discourses about public policies, with positive constructions leading to stronger popular support than negative constructions (Schneider and Ingram 1993), which can become an ideational source of self-undermining policy

---

[12] On the more general concept of social construction as it emerged in sociology, see Berger and Luckmann 1967.

feedback (Jacobs and Weaver 2015). These remarks about the social construction of target populations point to both the potential explanatory role of identity formation and the relationship between ideational processes and asymmetrical power relations, an issue discussed in the next section.

12 Ideas, Power, and Interests

The claim that ideas and power are closely related is hardly new, but greater systematic attention has been paid to their interaction in recent years (Béland 2010b; Béland, Carstensen, and Seabrooke 2016; Parsons 2016). One way to explore this interaction is to study the different ways in which ideas and power can interact. For instance, in a recent article, Martin Carstensen and Vivien Schmidt (2016, p. 318) discuss several patterns of interaction:

> *power through ideas*, understood as the capacity of actors to persuade other actors to accept and adopt their views through the use of ideational elements; *power over ideas*, meaning the imposition of ideas and the power to resist the inclusion of alternative ideas into the policy-making arena; and *power in ideas*, which takes place through the establishing of hegemony or institutions imposing constraints on what ideas are considered.

Although helpful, this typology does not draw a clear line between power and domination, two concepts that are frequently conflated (Morriss 2006).

Following Morriss (2006), we can understand political power as the capacity to impact outcomes ("power to"). The approach to power articulated in this Element is distinct from the one put forward by Michel Foucault (1982), who seldom emphasizes agency beyond resistance to power or clearly articulates the theoretical dichotomy between "power to" and "power over," understood here as domination. This Element instead starts from the perspective that power (as "power to") is analytically distinct from domination (as "power over"), which Morriss (2006, p. 64) defines as "the power of some *over* others". The relationship between power and domination is a key analytical issue and we should recognize that "power to" can lead to domination. In fact, contrary to what Morriss (2006, p. 126) argues, as far as political power is concerned, the capacity to shape outcomes and "the ability to affect others" are closely related. This is true because, at least in liberal democracies, political power is largely about collective action, which involves coordination efforts and "the ability to affect others." As Hannah Arendt (1972, p. 143) suggests, political power "corresponds to the human ability not just to act but to act in concert." This vision of political power is insightful because it points to the collective nature of political power and mobilization. Yet, in contrast with Arendt's view, any acceptable definition of power should stress the fact that power resources (i.e., resources that allow actors to act together to reach their desired political goals) are unequally distributed. Placing inequality at the centre of the definition of political power is the best way to recognize that "power to" can lead to domination, which is a particular form of inequality.

This discussion raises theoretical issues about the concept of interests, which is closely associated with power and domination in the literature. For instance, in his widely cited book *Power: A Radical View*, Steven Lukes (2005, p. 27) stresses the existence of a strict opposition between subjective and material interests:

> A may exercise power over B by getting him to do what he does not want to do, but he also exercises power over him by influencing, shaping or determining his very wants. Indeed, is it not the supreme exercise of power to get another or others to have the desires you want them to have – that is, to secure their compliance by controlling their thoughts and desires?[13]

This statement is problematic because it assumes that the existence of objective, material interests stemming from the institutional and structural position of actors can be entirely separated from the perceptions of these actors. The separation between the logic-of-position and the logic-of-interpretation (Parsons 2007) illustrates the tensions internal to the concept of interests, which requires analytical development.

This is the case in part because, despite the fact that the economic and institutional position of political actors affects the configuration of their interests, two actors who occupy the same basic economic and institutional position can have contrasting interpretations of what their interests are (King 1973). According to Mark Blyth (2002), this situation is even more common during periods of economic, social, and political uncertainty, when well-established institutions are less likely to guide political actors' decisions. This remark points to the broader claim that ideational processes help actors define their interests, an idea that is consistently present in the literature about the role of ideas in public policy (Blyth 2002; Hay 2011; Jenson 1989; King 1973; Rodrik 2014; Schmidt 2011; Stone 2012; Weir 1992; Wendt 1999). For instance, as Hay (2011, p. 79) suggests, "Conceptions of self-interest provide a cognitive filter through which the actor orients himself or herself towards his or her

---

[13] Lukes (2005) draws on the work of political scientists Peter Bachrach and Morton S. Baratz, who argue that power has two faces: direct participation in the policy-making process and the creation or the reinforcement of "social and political values and institutional practices that limit the scope of the political process to public consideration of only those issues which are comparatively innocuous" to actors behind this creation or reinforcement (Bachrach and Baratz 1962: 948). Lukes (2005) supplements these two faces of power with a third dimension: the ideological capacity to shape misleadingly the preferences of other actors in order to reinforce one's domination.

environment, providing one (of several) means by which an actor evaluates the relative merits of contending potential courses of action." One can argue that such a "cognitive filter" concerns both self-perceptions and the framing processes that actors use to convince others that it is in their interest to mobilize to reach shared goals and have an impact on outcomes.

David Marsh (2009, p. 6) criticizes the work of scholars such as Hay (2006) and claims that, in studying interests and politics more generally, scholars should "recognise that the relationship between the material and the ideational, like that between structure and agency, is dialectical, that is interactive and iterative." Accusing Hay (2006) of going too far in his constructivist understanding of interests, Marsh (2009, p. 689) claims that "the material reality has an effect on ... discourse" and that, as a consequence, interests are not purely ideational in nature. The more general point here is that, although perceived through actors' ideas, interests are not purely subjective, and that the logic-of-interpretation associated with their ideas interacts with the logic-of-position, which features both structural and institutional factors (Parsons 2007). This systematic attention to institutions is missing from Marsh's account. This is problematic because there is strong evidence that an actor's institutional position can impact their perceived interests and mobilization strategies. For example, scholarship on the power of US businesses suggests that political institutions such as federalism have a direct impact on business organizations' preferences and political strategies (Hacker and Pierson 2002). This is why, from an ideational and institutional perspective, any discussion about interests should take into account both actors' ideational *interpretations* and their structural and institutional *position*.

At the same time, the analysis of power relations requires paying close attention to coalition building as it intersects with institutional and ideational processes. This is the case because, if political power involves a capacity to "act in concert" (Arendt 1972, p. 143), then bringing people together is an essential task for policy entrepreneurs and other political actors. Institutions impact coalition building in at least three major ways. First, electoral and parliamentary rules shape party systems which, in turn, impact the ways in which political coalitions rise and fall. For instance, compared to the situation prevailing in other democracies, US political institutions make it difficult for third parties to emerge, which has direct consequences for coalition building within concrete policy areas (Maioni 1998). Second, as suggested earlier, institutional veto points can shape the mobilization of key interest groups, which has a direct influence on coalition building within the policy process (Immergut 1992). Finally, as the policy feedback literature suggests, existing policy legacies can directly affect political mobilization and coalition building (Campbell 2003).

Ideas participate in coalition building in at least three major ways. First, as Sabatier (1988) suggests, core beliefs can help keep advocacy coalitions together. From this perspective, shared values and assumptions keep coalitions together. Second, policy entrepreneurs and other political actors can use framing processes to shape the perceived interests of key constituencies as a way to bring or keep people together (Campbell 2004). What these actors typically do is convey the message that a certain policy alternative is consistent with the perceived interests of groups and individuals by appealing directly to them and suggesting that it is in their interest to support that policy alternative. For instance, policy experts and politicians can write op-eds and Tweets telling younger citizens that, in a context of demographic aging, existing public pension systems are soon going to go bankrupt and that younger people should pressure policy-makers to replace these systems with personal savings accounts, which are described as consistent with the long-term economic interests of this segment of the population (Teles 1998). Finally, political actors can gather around broader, more abstract policy ideas that have a positive meaning and a high level of valence (Cox and Béland 2013), which helps these ideas act as "coalition magnets" (Béland and Cox 2016). Characteristics of ideas that can act as coalition magnets include ambiguity because policy ideas, such as sustainability and solidarity, are likely to appeal to a range of different people for different reasons (Jenson 2010; Palier 2005). This means that the characteristics of a particular policy idea can have an impact on coalition building. At the same time, policy entrepreneurs are necessary to move these ideas onto the policy agenda and to frame them in a way that appeals to different groups and individuals (Béland and Cox 2016). From an ideational and institutional perspective, a promising avenue for future research would be to examine how ideas as coalition magnets interact with the institutional factors discussed earlier to shape coalition building and the power relations surrounding particular policies. This points once again to the relationship between ideational and institutional processes, explored further in the next section through a discussion about the production of expertise.

13 Institutions and the Production of Expertise

The production of expertise is central to contemporary policy-making. The rise of expertise in modern societies is related to an increasingly complex division of labour according to which specialized knowledge becomes necessary to the functioning of organizations and the formulation and evaluation of policies. Expertise is so central to contemporary societies that authors such as Tom

Nichols (2017) warn about the negative consequences of a potential "death of expertise" related to a growing societal distrust towards experts and their advice. Yet, regardless of what citizens might think of experts and their knowledge, expertise remains essential to contemporary policy-making (for a critical perspective, see Fischer 2003).

The institutionalist literature suggests that the production of expertise, which is an ideational reality, relates directly to institutional processes, as cross-national differences in state and political institutions explain why some sources of expertise are more or less prevalent in each country (Campbell and Pedersen 2014; Hall 1989). The contrast between France and the United States can illustrate these differences in the institutionalization of expertise (Béland and Viriot Durandal 2003). In the context of a centralized and unitary state, France is characterized by a statist model of expertise in which civil servants and public-sector organizations are the main and most legitimate sources of policy expertise (Restier-Melleray 1990). The United States, however, is characterized by a pluralist model of expertise where think tanks and other civil society organizations are central to the production of policy expertise. This is partly a result of the fragmented nature of US political and policy institutions that grants direct outside access to policy-makers (Restier-Melleray 1990; Rich 2004). Conversely, think tanks are much less influential in France, where state-centric expertise has long dominated (Desmoulins 2000).

These institutional differences in the production of expertise lead to the crystallization of what John L. Campbell and Ove K. Pedersen (2011, 2014) call "knowledge regimes." According to them, the level of state centralization and openness in each country, combined with the nature of their economic institutions (liberal market economy versus coordinated market economy), produce a distinct knowledge regime that shapes the ways in which expertise is produced and legitimized. This institutionalist framework leads Campbell and Pedersen (2011, p. 186) to formulate a typology of four main knowledge regimes: a market-oriented regime (liberal market economy and decentralized, open state); a politically tempered knowledge regime (liberal market economy and centralized, closed state); a consensus-oriented knowledge regime (coordinated market economy and decentralized, open state); and a statist-technocratic knowledge regime (coordinated market economy and centralized, closed state). This approach to the production of expertise is original because it combines the analysis of state and political institutions associated with historical institutionalism with the "varieties of capitalism" approach in political economy, which focuses on economic institutions and the contrast between liberal market economies such as Canada and the United States and coordinated market economies such as Germany and Sweden (Hall and Soskice 2001).

Beyond knowledge regimes, scholars should also pay attention to the literature on "policy advisory systems" (Craft and Howlett 2013; Halligan 1995). According to Jonathan Craft and Michael Howlett (2013, p. 187), these systems "arise in almost every instance of decision-making whereby governments receive advice not just from professional analysts in their employ or from outside groups, but also from a range of other actors, from think tanks and lobbyists, but also from partisan political advisors, scientific, technical and legal experts, and many others both inside and outside of government." As in the knowledge regime literature (Campbell and Pedersen 2011, 2014), this quote highlights the importance of forms of expertise located both inside and outside the state. This is especially true given the emergence of the "new public administration," which has been associated with the rise of outside consultants and sources of expertise in policy reform, a phenomenon that varies from country to country based on existing institutional legacies (Saint-Martin 2000). Beyond these differences, in advanced industrial countries, state bureaucrats remain key providers of policy expertise and, under specific institutional conditions, can exert a great deal of ideational influence over policy-makers, including elected officials (Heclo 1974; Marier 2005).

The above Craft and Howlett (2013, p. 187) quote also points to the fact that, beyond the technical advice actors such as state bureaucrats and think tanks provide, there is a political side to offering advice to the government. This is a significant aspect of the politics of public policy, especially when elected officials are concerned. These officials hire political and communication advisors who help them develop new electoral strategies that involve framing the issues of the day and constructing the "need to reform" certain policies (Cox 2001). Such remarks stress the need to pay close attention to the electoral and framing strategies not only of policy-makers, but also of the political advisors who help them fight political and framing battles over the policy issues of the day (Campbell 2004; Craft 2016).

Finally, both the literature on knowledge regimes and the scholarship on policy advisory systems point to the need to pay close attention to the role of think tanks as external sources of advice for policy-makers. The vast literature on think tanks is relevant for the study of the role of ideas in public policy (McGann and Weaver 2000; Medvetz 2012; Rich 2004; Stone and Denham 2004). A fascinating trend discussed within this literature is the "politicization of expertise" (Rich and Weaver 1998) and the emergence of what R. Kent Weaver (1989) calls "advocacy tanks," which are distinct from contract-based research organizations and "universities without students." Especially prevalent in the United States, the politicization of expertise points to the reality that expertise can be hard to untangle from politics, just as evidence is sometimes hard to untangle from normative assumptions (Parkhurst 2017).

More generally, following the knowledge-regime approach, it is clear that political institutions and policy legacies shape expertise and help explain why and how the dominant sources of expertise vary from country to country. This historical institutionalist understanding of the production of expertise points to how ideas and institutions interact over time to shape the politics of public policy, which is hard to understand without paying close comparative attention to the production of expertise in each country.

14 Mechanisms of Policy Change

Like knowledge regimes and advisory systems, policies change over time, an issue that has become a central concern in recent studies and an unavoidable topic when studying the politics of public policy in contemporary societies (Campbell 2004; Hacker 2004; Mahoney and Thelen 2009; Palier 2002; Streeck and Thelen 2005; Thelen 2004). This is why it is helpful at this stage of the discussion to tackle this issue systematically in reaction to scholars such as Paul Pierson (2000), who have emphasized stability and path dependence over transformative change, which they depict as rare and typically the product of exogenous shocks. Beyond historical institutionalism, policy research dealing with punctuated equilibrium has also emphasized stability over transformative change, which has been seen as exceptional, occurring during rare critical junctures rather than manifesting itself in a continuous manner (Baumgartner and Jones 1993).

Many institutionalist scholars have explicitly reacted to this tendency, emphasizing the existence of incremental yet transformative forms of policy change that exist beyond critical junctures and the punctuated equilibrium framework (Campbell 2004; Hacker 2004; Mahoney and Thelen 2009; Palier 2002; Streeck and Thelen 2005; Thelen 2004). Within this new historical institutionalist scholarship, the works of Kathleen Thelen (2004) and Jacob Hacker (2004) are especially meaningful because they offer a systematic framework for analysing incremental yet transformative policy change. Focusing mainly on endogenous institutional factors rather than on exogenous structural factors (Pierson 2000) as the main source of policy change, these scholars and their collaborators explore various institutional mechanisms that help actors gradually bring about transformative change (Hacker 2004; Mahoney and Thelen 2009; Streeck and Thelen 2005; Thelen 2004). For example, in a seminal article, Hacker (2004, p. 248) draws a line between three mechanisms of incremental yet transformative policy change: layering, conversion, and policy drift. Although they coexist with other mechanisms (Campbell 2004), these three specific mechanisms are ever-present in the recent literature on incremental yet transformative policy change (Mahoney and Thelen 2009; Streeck and Thelen 2005).

First, layering concerns "the grafting of new elements onto an otherwise stable institutional framework," a situation that can gradually transform its trajectory over time (Thelen 2004, p. 35; on layering, see also Schickler 2001). Second, conversion refers to the internal transformation of policy institutions stemming from the ways in which political actors "actively exploit" their "inherent ambiguities" to steer them in a different direction, without formally eliminating or replacing them (Mahoney and Thelen 2009, p. 17). Third, policy drift describes the "transformation of stable policy due to changing circumstances" related to the absence of reforms capable of adapting exiting policy instruments to such a changing environment (Hacker 2004, p. 248). Beyond their incremental yet transformative nature, what these three mechanisms have in common is that political actors typically adopt them because the existing policies they seek to abolish or replace are politically resilient, forcing them to adopt more indirect measures and strategies to bring about transformative change gradually. This approach is distinct from the traditional understanding of incrementalism in public policy research, which sees incrementalism as the opposite of transformative change (Lindblom 1959). At the same time, although there is strong empirical evidence that the three mechanisms of incremental yet transformative policy change defined above may have a strong impact on existing policy legacies (Hacker 2004; Mahoney and Thelen 2009; Streeck and Thelen 2005; Thelen 2004), Hacker (2004, p. 248) stresses that revision – the "formal reform, replacement, or elimination of existing policy"– remains a crucial mechanism of policy change. This mechanism is not incremental in nature because it leads to rapid policy transformation.

Unfortunately, the study of the above mechanisms does not systematically explore the role of ideas in policy change (Béland 2007b; Béland and Waddan 2012). Although some ideational elements are implicitly present in the literature on incremental yet transformative policy change (Wincott 2011), a growing number of scholars are paying direct attention to the ideational side of these mechanisms (Béland 2007b; Béland and Waddan 2012; Bhatia 2010; Boothe 2015; Cox 1998; Kay 2007; Palier 2002). For instance, in *The Politics of Policy Change*, Daniel Béland and Alex Waddan (2012) demonstrate how analysing key actors' ideas is necessary to explain why and how they turn to the above policy-change mechanisms. In their discussion of US Social Security, they show how the emergence of pension privatization as a policy idea shaped the layering strategies of conservative political actors seeking to bring about policy change gradually within this specific policy area (Béland and Waddan 2012). What this example suggests is that ideas shape the ways in which actors choose, perceive, and use mechanisms of policy change. This is yet another way in which ideational and institutional factors – in this case, concrete mechanisms of institutional change – interact to produce policy change, a concept that must be clearly defined. For instance, if policy change is defined mainly in terms of changes to institutional rules and norms, as is the case within historical institutionalism, researchers must say so. If they do not, the lack of a clear definition of what is to be explained (in this case, policy change) leads to the well-known "dependent variable problem" in policy research (Clasen and Siegel 2007; see also Daigneault 2014). This is why scholars must define what types of policy change they seek to explain before looking at the potential mechanisms actors might use to bring about change in the first place (Béland and Waddan 2012; Quadagno and Street 2006).

The institutionalist literature on incremental yet transformative change should not hide the fact that ideas, just like institutions, are not as stable as they may appear (Carstensen 2010). Drawing on the work of political theorists Ernesto Laclau and Chantal Mouffe (1985), Martin Carstensen (2010) suggests that ideas are dynamic realities that constantly change as their internal components evolve over time. He uses this dynamic understanding of ideational change to criticize approaches such as the advocacy coalition framework (Sabatier and Jenkins-Smith 1993), which, he argues, overemphasizes the stability of policy actors' core norms and beliefs (Carstensen 2010, p. 598). Carstensen's (2010) work is a useful reminder that emphasizing change should address both ideas and institutions, neither of which should be theorized as overly stable and coherent. At the same time, future research could look into whether some types of ideas are more stable and coherent than others. For instance, are framing processes more changing and dynamic than the public sentiments they seek to alter? In this regard, there is strong evidence that public sentiments are relatively stable over time (Brooks and Manza 2007) while framing activities involve the combination of various ideational elements in what is known as "bricolage" (Campbell 2004, p. 103).

The concept of bricolage is particularly interesting because it provides scholars with yet another mechanism with which to theorize policy change at both the institutional and the ideational levels (Campbell 2004; Carstensen 2011). On the one hand, Campbell (2004, p. 69) theorizes bricolage as a mechanism of institutional change through which policy actors can "craft new institutional solutions by recombining" existing elements into "new institutions [that] differ from but resemble old ones." There are two main forms of bricolage: substantive bricolage, which is an instrumental recombination of institutional policy elements to address new policy programs; and symbolic bricolage, which is ideational in nature and concerns the framing of new policy solutions in culturally appropriate ways (Campbell 2004: 69–70). This is typically done by drawing on existing symbols and values to increase the apparent cultural legitimacy of new policy solutions (Campbell 2004, p. 70). On the other hand, Carstensen (2011, p. 147) understands bricolage as a specific type of agency "where bits and pieces of the existing ideational and institutional legacy are put together in new forms leading to significant political transformation." Much less focused on coherence than what Carstensen (2011) sees as the alternative type of agency associated with the concept of policy paradigm (Hall 1993), bricolage is highly relevant for the topic of the present Element because it has clear ideational and institutional components. Future empirical research needs to further untangle these components so as to draw a clear analytical line between different explanatory logics (Parsons 2007) before exploring how they intersect. This specific remark about bricolage points once again to the broader issue of how different exploratory logics may interact and even become interdependent (Padamsee 2009) as they produce both stability and change over time.

The next section returns to this issue by bringing in structural and psychological explanations as they relate to, and potentially interact with, ideational and institutional explanations. As suggested, while explaining policy stability and change is often about the relationship between ideas and institutions, scholars would ignore structural and psychological factors at their peril.

15 Structural and Psychological Factors

Even when scholars focus primarily on the role of ideas and institutions and their interaction, they should not neglect structural and psychological factors. This is the case because, as Parsons (2007) suggests, scholars should keep in mind that if their preferred explanatory factors are unable to solve particular empirical puzzles on their own, they must turn to alternative types of explanation and assess whether they help solve such puzzles. Thus, scholars interested in the role of ideas and institutions must keep an eye on the potential impact of structural and psychological factors, especially when ideas and institutions seem unable to answer the research puzzle at hand. There is no universal answer to the question of whether and when these scholars should pay systematic attention to structural or psychological factors. This is an empirical question, and these factors can become central in particular contexts but not in others. Considering this, scholars working on ideas and institutions should always keep these in mind as potential explanatory factors even if their work focuses primarily on ideational and institutional processes.

A key question for these scholars to think about is how these alternative explanatory factors may interact with ideas and institutions to shape policy outcomes. The impact of structural factors is widely studied in policy research, and it is clear from the literature that economic crises have the power to weaken existing institutional legacies while facilitating the influence of new policy ideas and actors (Blyth 2002). This is why the timing of economic crises and other exogenous shocks can have a direct impact on the policy process, typically by weakening the dominant advocacy coalition and the policy ideas and institutions associated with it (Sabatier 1988). At the same time, the ways in which policy actors perceive and frame these exogenous shocks is essential, especially because these structural factors are likely to intersect with how these actors understand their interests, which are never purely static and are likely to be reassessed during periods of perceived crises (Blyth 2002).

Economic crises are only one possible example of how structural factors can impact how actors perceive their interests. Another example is the geographical location of natural resources and the ways in which these are related to existing ideational and institutional legacies (Lecours and Béland 2010). For example, in Canada the fact that Alberta is an oil-rich province is essential to understanding its political role within the country's federal system. At the same time, the politics of oil in Alberta and in Canada more generally is shaped by constitutional (institutional) settings that give all ten provinces control over natural resources such as oil, and by ideological considerations about "Western Alienation," an historical and ideational construction that emerged before oil was discovered in Alberta (Janigan 2012).

As for psychological factors, they have recently emerged as central to contemporary policy debates, a situation related to the growing influence of cognitive psychology in behavioural economics and policy research more broadly (Cairney and Weible 2017; Tomer 2017). This influence is illustrated by the popularity among both scholars and policy-makers of books such as *Nudge* by Richard Thaler and Cass Sunstein (2008). The authors draw on findings from cognitive psychology to formulate new solutions aimed at addressing various policy problems. Cognitive psychology can also help explain the behaviour and decisions of key policy actors in the study of the politics of public policy (Jones and Baumgartner 2005). Purely psychological explanations of political behaviour, however, are generally less common in contemporary social science research than ideational, institutional, and structural explanations (Parsons 2007).

This is why students of the politics of public policy who pay direct attention to psychological factors often explore their interaction with other types of explanation (Jones and Baumgartner 2005; Weyland 2008). For the present

Element, the work of Kurt Weyland (2008) is particularly relevant because it engages directly with historical institutionalist scholarship to develop a theory of policy change grounded in insight from cognitive psychology and the concept of "bounded rationality," initially formulated by Herbert Simon (1957). According to Weyland (2008), historical institutionalist scholars such as Pierson (2000) have relied too much on insight from mainstream economics and rational-choice theory to define how actors perceive and react to events, a situation that helps account for the emphasis these scholars place on path dependence. Instead, Weyland (2008, p. 286) rejects rational-choice theory and draws on prospect theory, an approach grounded in the fact that "psychologists consistently find that people who face the prospect of loss tend to take bold, drastic, and risky counter-measures." This is consistent with how Parsons (2007) defines psychological explanations. From the basis of this universal claim, Weyland (2008, p. 287) goes on to show that "risk seeking in the domain of losses can explain drastic rescue efforts mounted by political actors seeking to stem political decay and restore basic institutional functioning." As they seek policy solutions to achieve these "rescue efforts," policy-makers look at programs adopted in other countries. Yet, their assessment of these programs is shaped by the cognitive biases stemming from "bounded rationality." For example, as Weyland (2008, p. 292) puts it, policy-makers "draw excessively firm conclusions from small samples and short time frames, assuming that the initial stretch of experience is representative of long-term performance. By jumping to this conclusion, decision-makers overlook the role of chance factors that can boost or depress initial performance yet cancel out in the medium and long term." This means that both the decision to embrace radical policy change and the assessment of foreign policy solutions are grounded in psychological biases at odds with the vision of agency associated with rational-choice theory. By adopting a psychological approach within a broader institutionalist framework, Weyland (2008) suggests how psychological explanations can contribute to institutionalist thinking. At the same time, his approach does not draw a clear line between ideational and psychological explanations, which are sometimes hard to untangle. His work would thus gain from more direct engagement with the ideational literature. Conversely, scholars interested in ideas and institutions could gain from taking psychological factors more directly into account, especially when ideational and institutional factors alone are unable to explain key political patterns and policy decisions.

16 Conclusion

This Element has offered a critical reading of several literature streams that enrich our understanding of how ideational and institutional processes may shape the politics of public policy while leaving room for the agency of actors and the potential explanatory significance of psychological and structural factors. A core message of the Element is that, in order to study policy stability and change, it is appropriate to bring together the analysis of ideas and institutions while drawing a clear line between them. Such an analysis necessitates breaking down ideas and institutions into more specific categories, and taking into consideration other potential causal factors – in this case, structural and psychological explanations.

Beyond these general remarks, to move the ideational and institutional literature forward, scholars could further explore four key issues. First, regarding the above-mentioned territorial levels, more could be written about how ideas play a central role at the local and municipal levels. This is the case because most of the research on ideational processes and the ways in which they interact with institutional factors typically focuses on the national and transnational levels, rather than the local and municipal levels. That said, more ideational and institutional scholarship has emerged in recent years to explore local factors as they interact with national and transnational factors (e.g., Bradford 2016; Dilworth and Weaver forthcoming; Weaver 2016). Timothy Weaver's (2016) work on urban renewal and neoliberal enterprise zones provides a recent example of how to study ideational processes at the local level without losing sight of broader institutional and transnational processes.

Second, although the present Element has engaged primarily with approaches developed in advanced industrial countries, other parts of the world, including the Global South, are exceptionally interesting sites in which to analyse empirically the interaction among ideational and institutional factors, especially where the role of transnational actors and their relationship with domestic actors is acknowledged. This is true because the understanding of public policy in the Global South requires special attention to transnational actors and processes, something evident in the African context, for example (Béland et al. 2018; Foli 2016).

Third, although this Element does not focus on methodological issues, it is possible to acknowledge that, because of its historically minded nature, process tracing is well-adapted to ideational and institutional analysis (Bennett and Checkel 2015; Jacobs 2015). Process tracing requires a detailed and rigorous analysis of how key actors' ideas evolve over time and how these actors interact with the changing institutional environment in which they operate. This type of analysis involves a clear discussion of the ideational and institutional mechanisms that may shape policy stability and change over time. It also requires a close look at the available qualitative and quantitative evidence best suited to trace the development of ideas and institutions and explain how they can shape policy stability and change, potentially alongside psychological and structural factors. Though more work is needed on process tracing and using it to improve empirical research about ideational and institutional processes in the politics of public policy, excellent scholarship is already available (Bennett and Checkel 2015; Jacobs 2015).

Yet, process tracing is only one of many possible methods scholars can use to explore ideational and institutional processes and their interactions – for example, content analysis. More important, the use of both qualitative and quantitative methods is relevant for ideational and institutional analysis (Béland and Cox 2011b). As Bevir and Blakely (2018) suggest, what really matters is for scholars to have clear theoretical assumptions about the world and to use existing methods in ways that are consistent with these assumptions. For instance, students of ideational processes do not have to restrict themselves to content analysis, interviews, or ethnographical methods. They can use mass surveys and quantitative analysis to tackle some of their research puzzles, as long as they do it in a way that both reflects their core theoretical assumptions and effectively serves their research objectives. If they do this, to quote Bevir and Blakely (2018, p. 91), "they are free to creatively make use of whatever method best serves their research goals and purposes." This pragmatic and pluralist approach to research methods is one that students of ideas and institutions should embrace beyond methodological wars that too frequently divert researchers away from the crucial task of solving concrete theoretical and empirical puzzles.

Finally, theoretically and empirically, scholars should pay close attention to how ideational and institutional factors relate to one another, and how the boundaries between ideas and institutions can become fuzzy, at best. The work of Padamsee (2009), mentioned earlier, is particularly relevant here because it urges scholars to move beyond interaction effects to study the potential interdependence of explanatory factors, including ideas and institutions. According to her, the creation of new institutions is closely related to – and interdependent with – the ideas that are being institutionalized in the first place (Padamsee 2009, p. 427). This means that, in addition to paying attention to how explanatory factors interact, scholars could study the conditions under which they become so intertwined with one another that their impact depends on their mutual imbrication. Although Parsons (2007) is right to stress the need to draw clear analytical lines between explanatory factors, scholars also need to recognize the empirical messiness of ideas and institutions in concrete political and policy processes. Future ideational and institutional scholarship should seek to map these processes better while avoiding concealing their inherent complexity and the empirical challenges associated with the comparative, political, and historically minded analysis of policy stability and change.

References

Akerlof, G. A., and R. E. Kranton. (2010). *Identity Economics: How Our Identities Shape Our Work, Wages, and Well-being*, Princeton: Princeton University Press.

Amenta, E. (1998). *Bold Relief: Institutional Politics and the Origins of Modern Social Policy*, Princeton: Princeton University Press.

Arendt, H. (1972). *Crises of the Republic*, New York: Harvest Books.

Bacchi, C. (2012). Why study problematizations? Making politics visible. *Open Journal of Political Science*, 2(1): 1–8. http://file.scirp.org/pdf/OJPS 20120100003_72526218.pdf

Bachrach, P., and M. S. Baratz. (1962). Two faces of power. *The American Political Science Review*, 56(4): 947–952.

Bakhtin, M. M. (1981). *The Dialogic Imagination: Four Essays*, Austin: University of Texas Press.

Ban, C. (2016). *Ruling Ideas: How Global Neoliberalism Goes Local*, Oxford: Oxford University Press.

Bardach, E. (1977). *The Implementation Game. What Happens After a Bill Becomes a Law*, Cambridge, MA: MIT Press.

Baumgartner, F. R., and B. D. Jones. (1993). *Agendas and Instability in American Politics*, Chicago: University of Chicago Press.

Baumgartner, F. R., B. D. Jones, and P. B. Mortensen. (2018). Punctuated equilibrium theory: Explaining stability and change in public policymaking. In C. M. Weible and P. A. Sabatier, eds., *Theories of the Policy Process*, 4th edn. Boulder: Westview Press, pp. 55–101.

Béland, D. (2005). Ideas and social policy: An institutionalist perspective. *Social Policy & Administration*, 39(1): 1–18.

Béland, D. (2007a). *Social Security: History and Politics from the New Deal to the Privatization Debate*, updated paperback edn., Lawrence: University Press of Kansas.

Béland, D. (2007b). Ideas and institutional change in social security: Conversion, layering, and policy drift. *Social Science Quarterly*, 88(1): 20–38.

Béland, D. (2009). Ideas, institutions, and policy change. *Journal of European Public Policy*, 16(5): 701–718.

Béland, D. (2010a). Reconsidering policy feedback: How policies affect politics. *Administration & Society*, 42(5): 568–590.

Béland, D. (2010b). The idea of power and the role of ideas. *Political Studies Review*, 8(2): 145–154.

Béland, D. (2016a). Ideas and institutions in social policy research. *Social Policy & Administration*, 50(6): 734–750.

Béland, D. (2016b). Kingdon reconsidered: Ideas, interests and institutions in comparative policy analysis. *Journal of Comparative Policy Analysis*, 18(3): 228–242.

Béland, D. (2017). Identity, politics, and public policy. *Critical Policy Studies*, 11(1): 1–18.

Béland, D., M. B. Carstensen, and L. Seabrooke, eds. (2016). *Ideas, Political Power, and Public Policy*, London: Routledge [reprint of special issue of *Journal of European Public Policy*].

Béland, D., and R. H. Cox, eds. (2011a). *Ideas and Politics in Social Science Research*, New York: Oxford University Press.

Béland, D., and R. H. Cox. (2011b). Introduction: Ideas and politics. In D. Béland and R. H. Cox, eds., *Ideas and Politics in Social Science Research*. New York: Oxford University Press, pp. 3–20.

Béland, D., and R. H. Cox. (2016). Ideas as coalition magnets: Coalition building, policy entrepreneurs, and power relations. *Journal of European Public Policy*, 23(3): 428–445.

Béland, D, R. Foli, M. Howlett, M. Ramesh, and J. J. Woo. (2018). Instrument constituencies and transnational policy diffusion: The case of conditional cash transfers. *Review of International Political Economy*, 25(4): 463–482. DOI:10.1080/09692290.2018.1470548.

Béland, D., and J. S. Hacker. (2004). Ideas, private institutions, and American welfare state "exceptionalism": The case of Health and Old-Age Insurance, 1915–1965. *International Journal of Social Welfare*, 13(1): 42–54.

Béland, D., and M. Howlett. (2016). How solutions chase problems: Instrument constituencies in the policy process. *Governance*, 29(3): 393–409.

Béland, D., and A. Lecours. (2008). *Nationalism and Social Policy: The Politics of Territorial Solidarity*, Oxford: Oxford University Press.

Béland, D., and V. Ridde. (2016). Ideas and policy implementation: Understanding the resistance against free health care in Africa. *Global Health Governance*, X(3): 10–23.

Béland, D., and J.-P. Viriot Durandal. (2003). L'expertise comme pouvoir: le cas des organisations de retraités face aux politiques publiques en France et aux États-Unis. *Lien social et politiques*, 50: 105–123.

Béland, D., and A. Waddan. (2012). *The Politics of Policy Change: Welfare, Medicare, and Social Security Reform in the United States*, Washington, DC: Georgetown University Press.

Béland, D., and A. Waddan. (2015). Breaking down ideas and institutions: The politics of tax policy in the US and the UK. *Policy Studies*, 36(2): 176–195.

Benford, R. D., and D. A Snow. (2000). Framing processes and social movements: An overview and assessment. *Annual Review of Sociology*, 26: 611–639.

Bennett, A., and J. T. Checkel, eds. (2015). *Process Tracing: From Metaphor to Analytic Tool*, New York: Cambridge University Press.

Bennett, C. J., and M. Howlett (1992). The lessons of learning: Reconciling theories of policy learning and policy change. *Policy Sciences*, 25: 275–294.

Benz, A., and J. Broschek, eds. (2013). *Federal Dynamics: Continuity, Change, and the Varieties of Federalism*, Oxford: Oxford University Press.

Berger, P. L., and T. Luckmann. (1967). *The Social Construction of Reality: A Treatise in the Sociology of Knowledge*, New York: Penguin Books.

Berman, S. (1998). *The Social Democratic Moment: Ideas and Politics in the Making of Interwar Europe*, Cambridge, MA: Harvard University Press.

Berman, S. (2006). *The Primacy of Politics: Social Democracy and the Ideological Dynamics of the Twentieth Century*, New York: Cambridge University Press.

Berman, S. (2011). Ideology, history and politics. In D. Béland and R. Cox, eds., *Ideas and Politics in Social Science Research*. New York: Oxford University Press, pp. 105–126.

Berman, S. (2013). Ideational theorizing in political science: The evolution of the field since Peter Hall's "policy paradigms, social learning and the state." *Governance*, 23(6): 217–237.

Bevir, M., and J. Blakely (2018). *Interpretative Social Science: An Anti-Naturalist Approach*. Oxford: Oxford University Press.

Bevir, M., and R. A. W. Rhodes. (2003). *Interpreting British Governance*, London: Routledge.

Bhatia, V. (2010). Social rights, civil rights, and health reform in Canada. *Governance*, 23(1): 37–58.

Bhatia, V., and W. Coleman. (2003). Ideas and discourse: Reform and resistance in the Canadian and German health systems. *Canadian Journal of Political Science*, 36(4): 715–739.

Bleich, E. (2003). *Race Politics in Britain and France: Ideas and Policymaking since the 1960s*, New York: Cambridge University Press.

Blyth, M. (1997). Any more bright ideas? The ideational turn of comparative political economy. *Comparative Politics*, 29(2): 229–250.

Blyth, M. (2002). *Great Transformations: Economic Ideas and Institutional Change in the Twentieth Century*, Cambridge: Cambridge University Press.

Blyth, M., O. Helgadottir, and W. Kring. (2016). Ideas and historical institutionalism. In O. Fioretos, T. G. Falleti, and A. Sheingate, eds., *The Oxford Handbook of Historical Institutionalism*. Oxford: Oxford University Press, pp. 142–162.

Bonoli, G. (2001). Political institutions, veto points, and the process of welfare state adaptation. In P. Pierson, ed., *The New Politics of the Welfare State*. Oxford: Oxford University Press, pp. 238–264.

Boothe, K. (2015). *Ideas and the Pace of Change: National Pharmaceutical Insurance in Canada, Australia, and the United Kingdom*, Toronto: University of Toronto Press.

Bourdieu, P. (1984). *Distinction: A Social Critique of the Judgment of Taste*, Cambridge, MA: Harvard University Press.

Bradford, N. (1998). *Commissioning Ideas: Canadian National Policy Innovation in Comparative Perspective*, Toronto: University of Toronto Press.

Bradford, N. (2016). Ideas and collaborative governance: A discursive localism approach. *Urban Affairs Review*, 52(5): 659–684.

Brooks, C., and J. Manza. (2007). *Why Welfare States Persist: The Importance of Public Opinion in Democracies*, Chicago: University of Chicago Press.

Campbell, A. L. (2003). *How Policies Make Citizens: Senior Political Activism and the American Welfare State*, Princeton: Princeton University Press.

Campbell, A. L. (2012). Policy makes mass politics. *Annual Review of Political Science*, 15: 331–351.

Campbell, J. L. (2002). Ideas, politics, and public policy. *Annual Review of Sociology*, 28: 21–38.

Campbell, J. L. (2004). *Institutional Change and Globalization*. Princeton: Princeton University Press.

Campbell, J. L., and O. K. Pedersen. (2011). Knowledge regimes and comparative political economy. In D. Béland and R. H. Cox, eds., *Ideas and Politics in Social Science Research*. New York: Oxford University Press, pp. 167–190.

Campbell, J. L., and O. K. Pedersen. (2014). *The National Origins of Policy Ideas Knowledge Regimes in the United States, France, Germany, and Denmark*. Princeton: Princeton University Press.

Cairney, P., and C. M. Weible. (2017). The new policy sciences: Combining the cognitive science of choice, multiple theories of context, and basic and applied analysis. *Policy Sciences*, 50(4): 619–627.

Capano, G., and M. T. Galanti. (2018). Policy dynamics and types of agency: From individual to collective patterns of action. *European Policy Analysis*, 4(1): 23–47.

Carstensen, M. B. (2010). Ideas are not as stable as political scientists want them to be: A theory of incremental ideational change. *Political Studies*, 59(3): 596–615.

Carstensen, M. B. (2011). Paradigm man vs. the bricoleur: An alternative vision of agency in ideational change. *European Political Science Review*, 3(1): 147–167.

Carstensen, M. B., and V. A. Schmidt. (2016). Power through, over and in ideas: Conceptualizing ideational power in discursive institutionalism. *Journal of European Public Policy*, 23(3): 318–337.

Chwieroth, J. M. (2010). *Capital Ideas: The IMF and the Rise of Financial Liberalization*, Princeton: Princeton University Press.

Clasen, J., and N. A. Siegel. (2007). Comparative welfare state analysis and the "dependent variable problem." In J. Clasen and N. A. Siegel, eds., *Investigating Welfare State Change: The "Dependent Variable Problem" in Comparative Analysis*. Cheltenham: Edward Elgar, pp. 3–12.

Coleman, W. D., G. D. Skogstad, and M. M. Atkinson. (1996). Paradigm shifts and policy networks: Cumulative change in agriculture. *Journal of Public Policy*, 16(3): 273–301.

Cox. R. H. (1998). The consequences of welfare reform: How conceptions of social rights are changing. *Journal of Social Policy*, 26(1): 1–16

Cox, R. H. (2001). The social construction of an imperative: Why welfare reform happened in Denmark and the Netherlands but not in Germany. *World Politics*, 53: 463–498.

Cox, R. H., and D. Béland. (2013). Valence, policy ideas and the rise of sustainability. *Governance*, 26(2): 307–328.

Craft, J. (2016). *Backrooms and Beyond: Partisan Advisers and the Politics of Policy Work in Canada*, Toronto: University of Toronto Press.

Craft, J., and M. Howlett. (2013). The dual dynamics of policy advisory systems: The impact of externalization and politicization on policy advice. *Policy and Society*, 32(3): 187–197.

Daigneault, P.-M. (2014). Reassessing the concept of policy paradigm: Aligning ontology and methodology in policy studies. *Journal of European Public Policy*, 21(3): 453–469.

Daigneault, P.-M., and D. Béland. (2015). Taking explanation seriously in political science. *Political Studies Review*, 13(3): 384–392.

Deacon, B. (2007). *Global Social Policy and Governance*, London: Sage.

Desmoulins, L. (2000). French public policy research institutes and their political impact as another illustration of the French exception. In J. G. McGann and R. K. Weaver, eds., *Think Tanks and Civil Societies: Catalyst for Ideas and Action*. New York: Transaction Publishers, pp. 139–168.

Dilworth, R., and T. P. R. Weaver, eds. Forthcoming. *How Ideas Shape Urban Political Development*, Philadelphia: University of Pennsylvania Press.

Dobbin, F. (1994). *Forging Industrial Policy: The United States, Britain and France in the Railway Age*, New York: Cambridge University Press.

DiMaggio, P. J., and W. W. Powell. (1983). The Iron Cage revisited: Institutional isomorphism and collective rationality in organizational fields. *American Sociological Review*, 48(2): 147–160.

Dolowitz, D. P., and D. Marsh. (2000). Learning from abroad: The role of policy transfer in contemporary policy-making. *Governance*, 13(1): 5–23.

Dunlop, C., and C. Radaelli (2018). The lessons of policy learning: types, triggers, hindrances and pathologies. *Policy & Politics*, 46(2): 255–272.

Evans, P. B., D. Rueschemeyer, and T. Skocpol, eds. (1985). *Bringing the State Back In*, New York: Cambridge University Press.

Fearon, J. D. (1999). *What is Identity (As We Now Use the Word)?* Palo Alto: Stanford University.

Fenwick, T. B. (2015). *Avoiding Governors: Federalism, Democracy, and Poverty Alleviation in Brazil and Argentina*, South Bend: University of Notre Dame Press.

Fioretos, O., T. G. Falleti, and A. Sheingate, eds. (2016). *The Oxford Handbook of Historical Institutionalism*, Oxford: Oxford University Press.

Fischer, F. (2003). *Reframing Public Policy: Discursive Politics and Deliberative Practices*, Oxford: Oxford University Press.

Foli, R. (2016). Transnational actors and policymaking in Ghana: The case of the Livelihood Empowerment Against Poverty. *Global Social Policy*, 16(3): 268–286.

Forbath, W. E. (1991). *Law and the Shaping of the American Labor Movement*, Cambridge, MA: Harvard University Press.

Foucault, M. (1982). The subject and power. *Critical Inquiry*, 8(4): 777–795.

Foucault, M. (1997). Polemics, politics and problematizations: An Interview with Michel Foucault. In P. Robinow (ed.), *Ethics, Subjectivity and Truth [The Essential Works of Foucault* (Vol. 1), 1954–1984], New York: New Press, pp. 111–119.

Fraser, N., and L. Gordon. (1994). "Dependency" demystified: Inscriptions of power in a keyword of the welfare state. *Social Politics*, 1(1): 4–31.

Freeden, M. (1996). *Ideologies and Political Theory: A Conceptual Approach*, Oxford: Oxford University Press.

Freeden, M. (2003). *Ideology: A Very Short Introduction*, Oxford: Oxford University Press.

Freeden, M., L. T. Sargent, and M. Stears, eds. (2013). *The Oxford Handbook of Political Ideologies*, Oxford: Oxford University Press.

Ganghof, S. (2017). The empirical uses of theoretical models: The case of veto player theory. *Political Studies Review*, 15(1): 49–59.

Garritzmann, J. L. (2015). Attitudes towards student support: How positive feedback effects prevent change in the four worlds of student finance. *Journal of European Social Policy*, 25(2): 139–158.

Genieys, W., and M. Smyrl, eds. (2008). *Elites, Ideas, and the Evolution of Public Policy*, Basingstoke: Palgrave.

Gofas, A., and C. Hay, eds. (2009). *The Role of Ideas in Political Analysis: A Portrait of Contemporary Debates*, London: Routledge.

Goffman, E. (1974). *Frame Analysis: An Essay on the Organization of Experience*, Cambridge, MA: Harvard University Press.

Goldstein, J., and R. O. Keohane. (1993). Ideas and foreign policy: An analytical framework. In J. Goldstein and R. O. Keohane, eds., *Ideas and Foreign Policy: Beliefs, Institutions, and Political Change*. Ithaca: Cornell University Press, pp. 3–30.

Green-Pedersen, C., and S. Walgrave, eds. (2014). *Agenda Setting, Policies, and Political Systems: A Comparative Approach*, Chicago: University of Chicago Press.

Greer, S., D. Béland, A. Lecours, and K. Dubin (2019). *Putting Federalism in its Place*. Unpublished book manuscript.

Gusfield, J. R. (1980). *The Culture of Public Problems: Drinking-Driving and the Symbolic Order*, Chicago: University of Chicago Press.

Haas, P. M. (1992). Introduction: Epistemic communities and international policy coordination. *International Organization*, 46(1): 1–35.

Hacker, J. S. (1997). *The Road to Nowhere: The Genesis of President Clinton's Plan for Health Security*, Princeton: Princeton University Press.

Hacker, J. S. (2004). Privatizing risk without privatizing the welfare state: The hidden politics of welfare state retrenchment in the United States. *American Political Science Review*, 98: 243–260.

Hacker, J. S., and P. Pierson. (2002). Business power and social policy: Employers and the formation of the American welfare state. *Politics and Society* 30(2): 277–325.

Hajer, M. A. (1995). *The Politics of Environmental Discourse: Ecological Modernization and the Policy Process*, Oxford: Oxford University Press.

Hall, P. A. (1986). *Governing the Economy: The Politics of State Intervention in Britain and France*, Oxford: Oxford University Press.

Hall, P. A. (1989). Introduction. In P. A. Hall, ed., *The Political Power of Economic Ideas: Keynesianism across Nations*. Princeton: Princeton University Press, pp. 1–26.

Hall, P. A. (1993). Policy paradigms, social learning and the state: The case of economic policymaking in Britain. *Comparative Politics*, 25(3): 275–296.

Hall, P. A., and D. Soskice, eds. (2001). *Varieties of Capitalism: The Institutional Foundations of Comparative Advantage*, Oxford: Oxford University Press.

Hall, P. A., and R. C. R. Taylor. (1996). Political science and the three new institutionalisms. *Political Studies*, 44(5): 936–957.

Halligan, J. (1995). Policy advice and the public sector. In B. G. Peters and D. T. Savoie, eds., *Governance in a Changing Environment*. Montréal and Kingston: McGill-Queen's University Press, pp. 138–172.

Hansen, R., and D. King. (2001). Eugenic ideas, political interests, and policy variance: Immigration and sterilization policy in Britain and the US. *World Politics*, 53(2): 237–263.

Hattam, V. C. (1993). *Labor Visions and State Power: The Origins of Business Unionism in the United States*, Princeton: Princeton University Press.

Hay, C. (2006). Constructivist institutionalism. In S. A. Binder, R. A. W. Rhodes, and B. A. Rockman, eds., *The Oxford Handbook of Political Institutions*. Oxford: Oxford University Press, pp. 56–74.

Hay, C. (2011). Ideas and the construction of interests. In D. Béland and R. H. Cox, eds., *Ideas and Politics in Social Science Research*. New York: Oxford University Press, pp. 65–82.

Hay, C., and D. Wincott. (1998). Structure, agency and historical institutionalism. *Political Studies*, 46(5): 951–957.

Heclo, H. (1974). *Modern Social Politics in Britain and Sweden: From Relief to Income Maintenance*, New Haven: Yale University Press.

Hogan, J., and M. Howlett, eds. (2015). *Policy Paradigms in Theory and Practice: Discourses, Ideas and Anomalies in Public Policy Dynamics*, New York: Palgrave.

Hood, R., and C. Hoyle. (2015). *The Death Penalty: A Worldwide Perspective*, 5th edn., Oxford: Oxford University Press.

Howlett, M., and I. Mukherjee, (2014). Policy design and non-design: Towards a spectrum of policy formulation types. *Politics and Governance*, 2(2): 57–71.

Howlett, M., M. Ramesh, and A. Perl. (2009). *Studying Public Policy: Policy Cycles and Policy Subsystems*, 3rd edn., Toronto: Oxford University Press.

Huddy, L., and A. Bankert. (2017). Political partisanship as a social identity. In W. R. Thompson, ed., *Oxford Research Encyclopedia of Politics*. Oxford: Oxford University Press, http://politics.oxfordre.com/view/10.1093/acrefore/9780190228637.001.0001/acrefore-9780190228637-e-250

Immergut, E. M. (1992). *Health Politics: Interests and Institutions in Western Europe*, New York: Cambridge University Press.

Jacobs, A. M. (2009). How do ideas matter? Mental models and attention in German pension politics. *Comparative Political Studies*, 42(2): 252–279.

Jacobs, A. M. (2011). *Governing for the Long Term: Democracy and the Politics of Investment*, Cambridge: Cambridge University Press.

Jacobs, A. M. (2015). Process tracing the effects of ideas. In A. Bennett and J. T. Checkel, eds., *Process Tracing: From Metaphor to Analytic Tool.* New York: Cambridge University Press, pp. 41–73.

Jacobs, A. M., and R. K. Weaver. (2015). When policies undo themselves: Self-undermining feedback as a source of policy change. *Governance*, 28(4): 441–457.

Janigan, M. (2012). *Let the Eastern Bastards Freeze in the Dark: The West versus the Rest since Confederation*, Toronto: Knopf.

Jenkins-Smith, H. C., D. Nohrstedt, C. M. Weible, and K. Ingold. (2018). The Advocacy Coalition Framework: An overview of the research program. In C. M. Weible and P. A. Sabatier, eds., *Theories of the Policy Process*, 4th edn. Boulder: Westview Press, pp. 135–172.

Jenson, J. (1989). Paradigms and political discourse: Protective legislation in France and the United States before 1914. *Canadian Journal of Political Science*, 22(2): 235–258.

Jenson, J. (2010). Diffusing ideas for after neoliberalism: The social investment perspective in Europe and Latin America. *Global Social Policy*, 10(1): 59–84.

Jobert, B., and P. Muller. (1987). *L'État en action: politique publiques et corporatismes*, Paris: Presses Universitaires de France.

Jones, B. D., and F. R. Baumgartner. (2005). *The Politics of Attention: How Government Prioritizes Problems*, Chicago: University of Chicago Press.

Kay, A. (2007). Tense layering and synthetic policy paradigms: The politics of health insurance in Australia. *Australian Journal of Political Science*, 42(4): 579–591.

Kay, A. (2005). A critique of the use of path dependency in policy studies. *Public Administration*, 8(3): 553–571.

Kay, S. J. (1999). Unexpected privatizations: Politics and social security reform in the Southern Cone. *Comparative Politics*, 31(4): 403–422.

King, A. (1973). Ideas, institutions and the policies of governments: A comparative analysis: Part III. *British Journal of Political Science*, 3(4): 409–423.

Kingdon, J. W. (2011) [1984]. *Agendas, Alternatives, and Public Policies*, updated 2nd edn., New York: Longman.

Laclau, E., and C. Mouffe. (1985). *Hegemony and Socialist Strategy: Towards a Radical Democratic Politics*, London: Verso.

Lamont, M., and V. Molnár. (2002). The study of boundaries in the social sciences. *Annual Review of Sociology*, 28: 167–195.

Lecours, A., ed. (2005). *New Institutionalism: Theory and Analysis*, Toronto: University of Toronto Press.

Lecours, A., and D. Béland. (2010). Federalism and fiscal policy: The politics of equalization in Canada. *Publius: The Journal of Federalism*, 40(4): 569–596.

Leff, M. H. (1983). "Taxing the 'Forgotten Man'": The Politics of Social Security Finance in the New Deal. *Journal of American History* 70(2): 359–379.

Lepsius, M. R. (2017). *Max Weber and Institutional Theory*, ed. Claus Wendt, Basel: Springer.

Lieberman, R. C. (2002). Ideas, institutions, and political order: Explaining political change, *American Political Science Review*, 96(4): 697–712.

Light, P. C. (1995). *Still Artful Work: The Continuing Politics of Social Security Reform*, New York: McGraw-Hill.

Lindblom, C. E. (1959). The science of "muddling through." *Public Administration Review*, 19(2): 79–88.

Lindquist, E., and A. Wellstead. (2018). "Causal mechanisms in policy process research: Are we taking them seriously? Should we?" Paper presented at the Toronto Public Policy and Governance Workshop, March 17, University of Toronto.

Lipsky, M. (2010) [1980]. *Street-Level Bureaucracy: Dilemmas of the Individual in Public Services*, 30th anniversary expanded edn., New York: Russel Sage Foundation.

Lowi, T. J. (1964). American business, public policy, case-studies, and political theory. *World Politics*, 16(4): 677–715.

Lukes, S. (2005). *Power: A Radical View*, 2nd edn., Basingstoke: Palgrave.

Lynch, J. (2006). *Age in the Welfare State: The Origins of Social Spending on Pensioners, Workers, and Children*, New York: Cambridge University Press.

Mahon, R., and S. McBride, eds. (2008). *The OECD and Transnational Governance*, Vancouver: UBC Press.

Mahoney, J. (2000). Path dependence in historical sociology. *Theory and Society*, 29(4): 507–548.

Mahoney, J., and K. Thelen, eds. (2009). *Explaining Institutional Change: Ambiguity, Agency, and Power*, New York: Cambridge University Press.

Maioni, A. (1998). *Parting at the Crossroads: The Emergence of Health Insurance in the United States and Canada*, Princeton: Princeton University Press.

Marier, P. (2005). Where did the bureaucrats go? Role and influence of the public bureaucracy in the Swedish and French pension reform debate. *Governance*, 18(4): 521–544.

Marsh, D. (2009). Keeping ideas in their place: In praise of thin constructivism. *Australian Journal of Political Science*, 44(4): 679–696.

McGann, J. G., and R. K. Weaver, eds. (2000). *Think Tanks and Civil Societies: Catalyst for Ideas and Action*, New York: Transaction Publishers.

McNamara, K. R. (1998). *The Currency of Ideas: Monetary Politics in the European Union*, Ithaca: Cornell University Press.

Medvetz, T. (2012). *Think Tanks in America*, Chicago: University of Chicago Press.

Mehta, J. (2011). The varied roles of ideas in politics: From "whether" to "how." In D. Béland and R. H. Cox, eds., *Ideas and Politics in Social Science Research*. New York: Oxford University Press, pp. 23–26.

Merrien, F.-X. (1997). *L'État-providence*, Paris: Presses Universitaires de France.

Mettler, S., and M. SoRelle. (2018). Policy feedback theory. In C. M. Weible and P. A. Sabatier, eds., *Theories of the Policy Process*, 4th edn. Boulder: Westview Press, pp. 103–134.

Mintrom, M., and J. Luetjens. (2017). Policy entrepreneurs and problem framing: The case of climate change. *Environment and Planning C: Politics and Space*, 35(8): 1362–1377.

Mintrom, M., and P. Norman. (2009), Policy entrepreneurship and policy change. *Policy Studies Journal*, 37(4): 649–667.

Morriss, P. (2006). Steven Lukes on the concept of power. *Political Studies Review*, 4(2): 124–135.

Müller, J.-W. (2016). *What is Populism?* Philadelphia: University of Pennsylvania Press.

Myles, J., and P. Pierson. (2001). The comparative political economy of pension reform. In P. Pierson, ed., *The New Politics of the Welfare State*. Oxford: Oxford University Press, pp. 305–333.

Nichols, T. (2017). *The Death of Expertise: The Campaign against Established Knowledge and Why it Matters*, Oxford: Oxford University Press.

North, D. C. (1990). *Institutions, Institutional Change, and Economic Performance*, New York: Cambridge University Press.

Noy, S. (2017). *Banking on Health: The World Bank and Health Sector Reform in Latin America*, New York: Palgrave.

Obinger, H., S. Leibfried, and F. G. Castles, eds. (2005). *Federalism and the Welfare State: New World and European Experiences*, Cambridge: Cambridge University Press.

Orenstein, M. A. (2008). *Privatizing Pensions: The Transnational Campaign for Social Security Reform*, Princeton: Princeton University Press.

Orloff, A. S. (1993). *The Politics of Pensions: A Comparative Analysis of Canada, Great Britain and the United States, 1880–1940*, Madison: University of Wisconsin Press.

Orren, K., and S. Skowronek (2004). *The Search for American Political Development*, New York: Cambridge University Press.

Ostrom, E. (1990). *Governing the Commons: The Evolution of Institutions for Collective Action*, Cambridge: Cambridge University Press.

Ouimet, M., R. Landry, S. Ziam, and P.-O. Bédard (2009), The absorption of research knowledge by public civil servants. *Evidence & Policy*, 5(4): 331–350.

Padamsee, T. (2009). Culture in connection: Re-contextualizing ideational processes in the analysis of policy development. *Social Politics*, 16(4): 413–445.

Palier, B. (2002). *Gouverner la sécurité sociale*, Paris: Presses Universitaires de France.

Palier, B. (2005). Ambiguous agreements, cumulative change: French social policy in the 1990s. In W. Streeck and K. Thelen, eds., *Beyond Continuity: Institutional Change in Advanced Political Economies*. New York: Oxford University Press, pp. 127–144.

Palier, B., and Y. Surel. (2005). Les "trois I" et l'analyse de l'État en action. *Revue française de science politique*, 55(1): 7–32.

Parkhurst, J. (2017). *The Politics of Evidence: From Evidence-Based Policy to the Good Governance of Evidence*, Abingdon: Routledge.

Parsons, C. (2002). Showing ideas as causes: The origins of the European Union. *International Organization*, 56(1): 47–84.

Parsons, C. (2007). *How to Map Arguments in Political Science*, Oxford: Oxford University Press.

Parsons, C. (2016). Ideas and power: Four intersections and how to show them. *Journal of European Public Policy*, 23(3): 446–463.

Peters, B. G. (2011). *Institutional Theory in Political Science: The New Institutionalism*, 3rd edn., London: Continuum.

Peters, B. G., J. Pierre, and D. S. King. (2005). The politics of path dependence: Political conflict in historical institutionalism. *Journal of Politics*, 67(4): 1275–1300.

Pfau-Effinger, B. (2005). Culture and welfare state policies: Reflections on a complex interrelation. *Journal of Social Policy*, 34(1): 3–20.

Pierson, P. (1993). When effect becomes cause: Policy feedback and political change. *World Politics*, 45(4): 595–628.

Pierson, P. (1994). *Dismantling the Welfare State? Reagan, Thatcher, and the Politics of Retrenchment*, New York: Cambridge University Press.

Pierson, P. (1995). Fragmented welfare states: Federal institutions and the development of social policy. *Governance*, 8(4): 449–478.

Pierson, P. (2000). Increasing returns, path dependence, and the study of politics. *American Political Science Review*, 94(2): 251–267.

Polletta, F., and J. M. Jasper. (2001). Collective identity and social movements. *Annual Review of Sociology*, 27: 283–305.

Pressman, J. L., and A. Wildavsky (1984). *Implementation: How Great Expectations in Washington Are Dashed in Oakland; Or, Why It's Amazing that Federal Programs Work at All, This Being a Saga of the Economic Development Administration as Told by Two Sympathetic Observers Who Seek to Build Morals on a Foundation of Ruined Hopes* (3rd edn). Berkeley: University of California Press.

Quadagno, J., and D. Street. (2006). Recent trends in US social welfare policy: Minor retrenchment or major transformation? *Research on Aging*, 28(3): 303–316.

Rayner, J. (2015). Is there a fourth institutionalism? Ideas, institutions and the explanation of policy change. In J. Hogan and M. Howlett (eds.), *Policy Paradigms in Theory and Practice: Discourses, Ideas and Anomalies in Public Policy Dynamics*, New York: Palgrave, pp. 61–80.

Restier-Melleray, C. (1990). Experts et expertise scientifique: Le cas de la France. *Revue française de science politique*, 40(4): 546–585.

Rich, A. (2004). *Think Tanks, Public Policy, and the Politics of Expertise*. Cambridge: Cambridge University Press.

Richards, R. (1994). *Closing the Door to Destitution: The Shaping of the Social Security Acts of the United States and New Zealand*. University Park: Pennsylvania State University Press.

Rich, A., and R. K. Weaver. (1998). Advocates and analysts: Think tanks and the politicization of expertise in Washington. In A. Cigler and B. Loomis, eds., *Interest Group Politics*, 5th edn. Washington, DC: Congressional Quarterly Press, pp. 235–253.

Roberts, N. C., and P. J. King (1991), Policy entrepreneurs: Their activity structure and function in the policy process. *Journal of Public Administration Research and Theory*, 1(2): 147–175.

Rochefort, D. A., and R. W. Cobb, eds. (1994). *The Politics of Problem Definition: Shaping the Policy Agenda*, Lawrence: University Press of Kansas.

Rodrik, D. (2014). When ideas trump interests: Preferences, worldviews, and policy innovations. *Journal of Economic Perspective*, 28(1): 189–208.

Rose, R. (1991). What is lesson-drawing? *Journal of Public Policy*, 11(1): 3–30.

Sabatier, P. A. (1988). An advocacy coalition framework of policy change and the role of policy-oriented learning therein. *Policy Sciences*, 21(2/3): 129–168.

Sabatier, P. A., and H. C. Jenkins-Smith, eds. (1993). *Policy Change and Learning: An Advocacy Coalition Approach*, Boulder: Westview Press.

Saint-Martin, D. (2000). *Building the New Managerialist State: Consultants and the Politics of Public Sector Reform in Comparative Perspective*, Oxford: Oxford University Press.

Schattschneider. E. E. (1935). *Politics, Pressures and the Tariff*, New York: Prentice-Hall.

Schickler, E. (2001). *Disjointed Pluralism: Institutional Innovation and the Development of the US Congress*, Princeton: Princeton University Press.

Schlager, E. (1995). Policy making and collective action: Defining coalitions within the Advocacy Coalition Framework. *Policy Sciences*, 28(3): 243–270.

Schlager, E, and M. Cox. (2018). The IAD Framework and the SES Framework: An introduction and assessment of the Ostrom Workshop Frameworks. In C. M. Weible and P. A. Sabatier, eds., *Theories of the Policy Process*, 4th edn. Boulder: Westview Press, pp. 215–252.

Schmidt, V. A. (2002a). Does discourse matter in the politics of welfare state adjustment? *Comparative Political Studies*, 35(2): 168–193.

Schmidt, V. A. (2002b). *The Futures of European Capitalism*. Oxford: Oxford University Press.

Schmidt, V. A. (2008). Discursive institutionalism: The explanatory power of ideas and discourse. *Annual Review of Political Science*, 11: 303–326.

Schmidt, V. A. (2011). Reconciling ideas and institutions through discursive institutionalism. In D. Béland and R. H. Cox, eds., *Ideas and Politics in Social Science Research*. New York: Oxford University Press, pp. 47–82.

Schneider, A., and H. Ingram. (1993). Social construction of target populations: Implications for politics and policy. *American Political Science Review*, 87(2): 334–347.

Schön, D. A., and M. Rein. (1994). *Frame Reflection: Toward the Resolution of Intractable Policy Controversies*, New York: Basic Books.

Shanahan, E. A., M. D. Jones, M. K. McBeth, and C. Radaelli. (2018). The narrative policy framework. In C. M. Weible and P. A. Sabatier, eds., *Theories of the Policy Process*, 4th edn. Boulder: Westview Press, pp. 173–214.

Sides, J., M. Tesler, and L. Vavreck. (2018). *Identity Crisis: The 2016 Presidential Campaign and the Battle for the Meaning of America*, Princeton: Princeton University Press.

Simon, H. A. (1957). *Models of Man, Social and Rational: Mathematical Essays on Rational Human Behavior in a Social Setting*, New York: John Wiley & Sons.

Skocpol, T. (1992). *Protecting Soldiers and Mothers: The Political Origins of Social Policy in the United States*, Cambridge, MA: The Belknap Press of the Harvard University Press.

Skogstad, G., ed. (2011). *Policy Paradigms, Transnationalism, and Domestic Politics*, Toronto: University of Toronto Press.

Somers, M., and F. Block. (2005). From poverty to perversity: Ideas, markets, and institutions over 200 years of welfare debate. *American Sociological Review*, 70(2): 260–287.

Soroka, S. N. (2002). *Agenda-Setting Dynamics in Canada*, Vancouver: UBC Press.

Steensland, B. (2008). *The Failed Welfare Revolution: America's Struggle over Guaranteed Income Policy*, Princeton: Princeton University Press.

Steinmo, S., and J. Watts. (1995). It's the institutions stupid! Why comprehensive health insurance always fails in America. *Journal of Health Politics Policy and Law*, 20(2): 329–372.

Steinmo, S., K. Thelen, and F. Longstreth, eds. (1992). *Structuring Politics: Historical Institutionalism in Comparative Analysis*, Cambridge: Cambridge University Press.

Stiller, Sabina. 2010. *Ideational Leadership in German Welfare State Reform: How Politicians and Policy Ideas Transform Resilient Institutions*, Amsterdam: Amsterdam University Press.

Stone, D. (2004). Transfer agents and global networks in the transnationalisation of policy. *Journal of European Public Policy*, 11(3): 545–566.

Stone, D. (2012). *Policy Paradox: The Art of Political Decision Making*, 3rd edn., New York: W. W. Norton.

Stone, D., and A. Denham, eds. (2004). *Think Tank Traditions: Policy Analysis across Nations*, Manchester: University of Manchester Press.

Streeck, W., and K. Thelen, eds. (2005). *Beyond Continuity: Institutional Change in Advanced Political Economies*, Oxford: Oxford University Press.

Svallfors, S. (2010). Policy feedback, generational replacement, and attitudes to state intervention: Eastern and Western Germany, 1990–2006. *European Political Science Review*, 2(1): 119–135.

Tarrow, S. (2005). *The New Transnational Activism*, Cambridge: Cambridge University Press.

Teles, S. (1998). "The dialectics of trust: Ideas, finance, and pension privatization in the US and the UK." Paper presented in October at the Annual

Meeting of the Association for Public Policy Analysis and Management (New York City).

Thaler, R. H., and C. R. Sunstein. (2008). *Nudge: Improving Decisions about Health, Wealth, and Happiness*, New York: Penguin Books.

Thelen, K. (2004), *How Institutions Evolve: The Political Economy of Skills in Germany, Britain, the United States, and Japan*, Cambridge: Cambridge University Press.

Tomer, J. F. (2017). *Advanced Introduction to Behavioral Economics*, Cheltenham: Edward Elgar.

Tsebelis, G. (2002). *Veto Players: How Political Institutions Work*, Princeton: Princeton University Press.

Tilly, C. (1998). *Durable Inequality*, Berkeley: University of California Press.

Tilly, C. (2005). *Identities, Boundaries, and Social Ties*, Boulder: Paradigm Publisher.

Voss, J.-P., and A. Simons. (2014). Instrument constituencies and the supply side of policy innovation: The social life of emissions trading. *Environmental Politics*, 23(5): 735–754.

Walsh, J. I. (2000). When do ideas matter? Explaining the successes and failures of Thatcherite ideas. *Comparative Political Studies*, 33(4): 483–516.

Weaver, R. K. (1989). The changing world of think tanks. *PS: Political Science & Politics*, 22(3): 563–578.

Weaver, R. K. (2010). Paths and forks or chutes and ladders: Negative feedbacks and policy regime change. *Journal of Public Policy*, 30(2): 136–162.

Weaver, T. (2016). *Blazing the Neoliberal Trail: Urban Political Development in the United States and the United Kingdom*, Philadelphia: University of Pennsylvania Press.

Weber, M. (1978) [1922]. *Economy and Society: An Outline of Interpretive Sociology*, Berkeley: University of California Press.

Weible, C. M., and P. A. Sabatier, eds. (2018). *Theories of the Policy Process*, 4th edn., Boulder: Westview.

Weible, C. M., P. A. Sabatier, H. C. Jenkins-Smith, D. Nohrstedt, A.D. Henry, and P. de Leon. (2011). A quarter century of the Advocacy Coalition Framework: An introduction to the special issue. *Policy Studies Journal*, 39(3): 349–360.

Weir, M. (1989). Ideas and politics: The acceptance of Keynesianism in Britain and in the United States. In P. A. Hall, ed., *The Political Power of Economic Ideas: Keynesianism across Nations*. Princeton: Princeton University Press, pp. 53–86.

Weir, M. (1992). *Politics and Jobs: The Boundaries of Employment Policy in the United States*, Princeton: Princeton University Press.

Wendt, A. (1999). *Social Theory of International Politics*, Cambridge: Cambridge University Press.

Weyland, K. (2008). Toward a new theory of institutional change. *World Politics*, 60(1): 281–314.

White, L. A. (2002). Ideas and the welfare state: Explaining child care policy development in Canada and the United States. *Comparative Political Studies*, 35(6): 713–743.

Wincott, D. (2011). Ideas, policy change and the welfare state. In B. Daniel and R. H. Cox, eds., *Ideas and Politics in Social Science Research*. New York: Oxford University Press, pp. 143–166.

Woods, N. (2006). *The Globalizers: The IMF, the World Bank, and their Borrowers*, Ithaca: Cornell University Press.

Wright Mills, C. (1959). *The Sociological Imagination*, New York: Oxford University Press.

Zohlnhöfer, R., N. Herweg, and C. Huß. (2016). Bringing formal political institutions into the multiple streams framework: An analytical proposal for comparative policy analysis. *Journal of Comparative Policy Analysis*, 18(3): 243–256.

Acknowledgements

The author acknowledges support from the Canada Research Chairs Program. He also thanks Robert Henry Cox, Pierre-Marc Daigneault, Michael Howlett, Angela Kempf, M. Ramesh, and Alex Waddan as well as the anonymous reviewers for their comments and suggestions. Some material in this Element is adapted from Béland 2016a and Béland 2010b.

About the Author

Daniel Béland is Director of the McGill Institute for the Study of Canada and James McGill Professor in the Department of Political Science at McGill University. A student of public policy from a comparative and historical perspective, he has published more than 15 books and 130 articles in peer-reviewed journals. Recent books include *Advanced Introduction to Social Policy* (with Rianne Mahon) and the *Oxford Handbook of US Social Policy* (co-edited with Christopher Howard and Kimberly J. Morgan).

Cambridge Elements ≡

Public Policy

M. Ramesh
National University of Singapore (NUS)
M. Ramesh is UNESCO Chair on Social Policy Design at the Lee Kuan Yew School of Public Policy, NUS. His research focuses on governance and social policy in East and Southeast Asia, in addition to public policy institutions and processes. He has published extensively in reputed international journals. He is Co-editor of *Policy and Society* and *Policy Design and Practice*.

Michael Howlett
Simon Fraser University, British Colombia
Michael Howlett is Burnaby Mountain Professor and Canada Research Chair (Tier 1) in the Department of Political Science, Simon Fraser University. He specialises in public policy analysis, and resource and environmental policy. He is currently editor-in-chief of *Policy Sciences* and co-editor of the *Journal of Comparative Policy Analysis; Policy and Society* and *Policy Design and Practice*.

David L. Weimer
University of Wisconsin-Madison
David L. Weimer is the Edwin E. Witte Professor of Political Economy, University of Wisconsin-Madison. He has a long-standing interest in policy craft and has conducted policy research in the areas of energy, criminal justice, and health policy. In 2013 he served as president of the Society for Benefit-Cost Analysis. He is a Fellow of the National Academy of Public Administration.

Xun WU
Hong Kong University of Science and Technology
Xun WU is Professor and Head of the Division of Public Policy at the Hong Kong University of Science and Technology. He is a policy scientist whose research interests include policy innovations, water resource management and health policy reform. He has been involved extensively in consultancy and executive education, his work involving consultations for the World Bank and UNEP.

Judith Clifton
University of Cantabria
Judith Clifton is Professor of Economics at the University of Cantabria, Spain. She has published in leading policy journals and is editor-in-chief of the *Journal of Economic Policy Reform*. Most recently, her research enquires how emerging technologies can transform public administration, a forward-looking cutting-edge project which received €3.5 million funding from the Horizon2020 programme.

Eduardo Araral

National University of Singapore (NUS)

Eduardo Araral is widely published in various journals and books and has presented in forty conferences. He is currently Co-Director of the Institute of Water Policy at the Lee Kuan Yew School of Public Policy, NUS and is a member of the editorial board of *Journal of Public Administration Research and Theory* and the board of the Public Management Research Association.

About the series

This series is a collection of assessments in the future of public policy research as well as substantive new research.

Edited by leading scholars in the field, the series is an ideal medium for reflecting on and advancing the understanding of critical issues in the public sphere. Collectively, the series provides a forum for broad and diverse coverage of all major topics in the field while integrating different disciplinary and methodological approaches.

Cambridge Elements ≡

Public Policy

Elements in the series

Printed in the United States
By Bookmasters